FROM JESUS TO JUDAISM

One Man's Search For A Meaningful Faith

SHLOMOH SHERMAN

The Reading Glass Books
1-888-420-3050
www.readingglassbooks.com
fulfillment@readingglassbooks.com

From Jesus To Judaism

One Man's Search For a Meaningful Faith
Shlomoh Sherman

Foreword by Rabbi Shlomo Riskin

A JEWISH VOICE CRYING OUT IN THE WILDERNESS OF AMERICA.

Shlomoh Sherman joined the traditional Jewish community the hard way, via Christianity. In his autobiographical odyssey, the author relates his experiences growing up in a non-religious Jewish home, how he became involved with the Hebrew Christians, why disenchantment set in, what frustrations he encountered from Jews in his efforts to join the religious Jewish community, and what made him turn to Judaism in spite of numerous rebuffs. As Rabbi Riskin notes. "By analyzing Mr. Sherman's experiences and observations, we can begin to understand what the American Jewish community must do to reach the many Jews who are at best indifferent to Judaism, and at worst, seriously alienated from it." This is a work that is sure to be a most valuable guide to those countless Jews who are looking for a path that will lead them to a meaningful Jewish lifestyle. Shlomoh Sherman lectures frequently on Jewish subjects including such topics as how Jews should respond to the threat posed by Christian missionaries, and what the organized Jewish community must do to reach the large numbers of uncommitted Jews.

Abraham Carmel writes:
Author, So Strange My Path

Mr. Sherman has performed an outstanding service to the Jewish community, and above all to our vulnerable youth. This project is an idea whose time has come, nay, rather, it is overdue.

To Shirley, Bernard, and Frances,

שפרה שרח בערל יצחק

ופרימע בני הערשל צבי בן אפריים

ובני טשארנע איטע בת שמואל הלוי

We are the children of those who, in the face of incredible adversity, continued to dream of the Messianic Era.

ACKNOWLEDGMENTS

I wish to express deepest appreciation and thanks to all those who helped make this book a reality:

Professor Shaye Cohen, who read the manuscript and whose thoughtful suggestions were incorporated; my friend, Rabbi David Freedman, with whom I discussed much of the material in the manuscript, who also offered valuable advice and who supplied me with much source material; my editors, John Vance, William Campbell, Carol Angelilli and Karen Scala who skillfully and professionally developed the manuscript; Reverend Father Matthew Borden, who also edited the manuscript critically from the viewpoint of a Christian clergyman, and who has become a very special friend to me and my family; Herbert Weiss, who patiently proofread the entire set of galleys with me; Amos Alter and Ron Nussbaum, who gave me the impetus to go ahead with the project; Gary Karshmer, who held my hand when the going got rough; my teacher and friend, Rabbi Shlomo Riskin, who graciously consented to write the Foreword; my teacher and friend, Rabbi Hirschel Cohen, a beautiful Jew, who invited me to his home for a *Shabbat* meal at the right time: my publisher, William Brandon, who believed that my manuscript was worth publishing and who decided to take a chance; Jessica Lopez, Marketing Consultant at ReadersMagnet, who considered my book relevant as a guide for any Jewish person seeking a meaningful relationship with his/her people, and who inspired me to have it republished under a more fitting title; Aime Ignacio, Author Relations Officer at ReadersMagnet, who tirelessly worked with me for many months, ensuring the accuracy of the text in its digital format; the members of The Reading Glass Books staff, dedicated to the success of this book; and last my beloved kinswoman (יין אחרון אחרון חביב) Pamela Elsa Milligan-Sherman (שרה עליה בת אברהם אבינו), who forced me to be honest.

I also wish to mention with great sadness, Professor Dr. Abraham Carmel, who graciously consented to write the Introduction. His recent passing is a loss for all of Israel.

Shlomoh Sherman

INTRODUCTION

I consider it a great privilege to be invited to write a brief introduction to *From Jesus To Judaism*.

Mr. Sherman has performed an outstanding service to the Jewish community, and above all to our vulnerable youth. This project is an idea whose time has come, nay, rather, it is overdue.

Hardly a week passes without my being called by some distraught Jewish parent or relative, whose loved one has been snatched by some missionizing zealot from the flames of hell fire and placed "safely" in the arms of Jesus.

In the near future, I shall thankfully be able to place Mr. Sherman's welcome volume in their hands.

Many qualities impressed me as I read and re-read the manuscript. Paramount among these was the transparent frankness and sincerity evident throughout. This frankness will appeal to a modern youth, impatient with reservations and diplomacy.

Mr. Sherman does not conceal his impatience with lukewarm rabbis who seem to care more about prestige than the welfare of our lost youth. I was delighted to read the warm tribute to Rabbi Riskin so richly merited. A hundred Rabbi Riskins could turn the tide of assimilation in America and ensure our future as a Jewish, *Torah*-oriented community.

As one who found Judaism from the outside, after many years of painful searching. I am strongly convinced that one *baal tsheshuva* is worth a thousand easily converted gentiles. Let our efforts be directed towards should-be Jews rather than would be Jews! Above all, let us embark upon a campaign to thwart the misguided efforts of the soul-snatchers!

Abraham Carmel

FOREWORD

In *From Jesus To Judaism*, Shlomoh Sherman tells us why Christianity once attracted him, the reasons he subsequently became disenchanted with it, and what caused his eventual turn to traditional Judaism. This stimulating and unusual odyssey relates how the author ultimately managed to avoid the Scylla of belief in a false messiah and the Charybdis of total disbelief. By analyzing Mr. Sherman's experiences and observations, we can begin to understand what the American Jewish community must do to reach the many Jews who are at best indifferent to Judaism, and at worst, seriously alienated from it.

Undoubtedly many Jews are not observant because contemporary society offers them such appealing but bewildering alternatives. Only those who will struggle to maintain their heritage and who have a sense of history are likely to withstand such temptations. To appreciate Judaism's inherent truths, we must first understand who we were and then become comfortable with what we are. At that point, we can become free to develop into what we want to be. It is such an investigation that Shlomoh made and which in some sense every reflective Jew must also undertake.

The Bible teaches: "Man does not live by bread alone but on that which goes forth from God's mouth." (*Deuteronomy 8*). In the *Targum Onkelos,* an Aramaic translation written more than 2,000 years ago, it is phrased "Not by bread alone does man exist, but by that which comes forth from God's mouth does man live. The stress is on the distinction between existence and essence. Mr. Sherman appreciates this. In his search, he came to realize that while material things are necessary to exist, they are not enough; to truly live, purpose, meaning, well being, and spiritual rootedness are equally essential.

On the Sabbath of *Hanukah*, 1964, Lincoln Square Synagogue was founded, and held its first service in an apartment on the West Side of Manhattan. Our raison d'être was to reach out to the many searching Jews who had an inchoate longing for the faith and moorings of the tradition. I am pleased to be able to say that Shlomoh Sherman was one of those we were able to assist. As he, himself, notes, it was the concern and guidance he was offered at Lincoln Square Synagogue that played so important a role in strengthening his commitment to Judaism. Over the years, we have been fortunate in assisting many to develop their Jewish awareness. This is an endeavor we would willingly share with the thousands of other synagogues throughout the country for the task is exceedingly great both in time and patience. It is not, however, an impossible one and Jewish communal leaders can learn much about how to proceed from Mr. Sherman's book. In particular, he urges affiliated Jews to take an interest in all strangers who wander into their synagogues, share Jewish experiences with them in a caring and personal way, and maintain a continuing interest in their spiritual as well as their other needs. By promoting such responsiveness, each congregation can be turned into a veritable kehillah, community, and this will surely result in its enhancement.

Shlomoh Sherman was fortunate to have discovered the essence of his Jewish heritage. Many, regretfully, do not. I am confident that this document of a personal journey to faith will serve as a remarkable guide for the countless Jews likely to embark on similar paths.

May it be God's will that many of these Jews be inspired by the words of this book! Let us pray that it will help them to re-establish ties with their past through adherence to the tradition, and in so doing secure their future, Israel's, and that of the world.

Rabbi Shlomo Riskin
New York, New York

If there arise among you a prophet,
Or a dreamer of dreams,
And giveth thee a sign or a wonder,
And the sign or the wonder come to pass,
Whereof he spoke unto thee, saying
Let us go after other gods,
Which thou hast not known, and let us serve them;
Thou shall not hearken unto the words of that prophet,
Or that dreamer of dreams...
Ye shall walk after the Lord your God,
And fear Him,
And keep His commandments,
And obey His voice,
And ye shall serve Him, and cleave unto Him.
And that prophet, or that dreamer of dreams,
Shall be put to death;
Because he hath spoken to turn you away from
The Lord your God,
Which brought you out of the land of Egypt,
And redeemed you out of the house of bondage.
To thrust thee out of the way
Which the Lord thy God commanded thee to walk in.
So shall thou put evil away from the midst of thee.

Deuteronomy 13:1-6

Contents

Part I

… Surely our fathers have inherited lies, vanity, and things wherein there is no profit.

Jeremiah 16:19

The wicked son says: What is this service to you? To you, and not to him. He thereby removes himself from the community and denies God.

Passover Haggadah

I
GOD
KILLER

I first encountered Jesus when I was six years old. I was born, the youngest of four children, in the Bronx, New York, on the ninth day of IYAR in the Jewish year 5697, which corresponds to April 20, 1937. The name on my birth certificate read Stanley Sherman. Eight days later I was circumcised in accordance with the precepts of the Jewish tradition. When the rabbi read the liturgical formula, "Our God and God of our fathers uphold this child for his father and his mother and let his name be called in Israel ..." my father answered "*Shloyme ben Hershl Zvi*," Solomon, son of Herschel Zvi.

I grew up on Charlotte Street, which is located in the Crotona Park section of the East Bronx. At that time it was an ethnically oriented Jewish neighborhood whose inhabitants were mainly immigrants from eastern Europe. My parents had come from Ukraine, and our home was bilingual, English and Yiddish. I remember being taken as a small child to visit my maternal grandfather in Brooklyn; on several occasions he took me with him when he went to services in a *shtibel*, a small Orthodox place of worship.

I attended P.S. 61, which today still stands on Charlotte Street between Boston Road and Crotona Park East. By the time I reached the first grade, I was able to understand that Jews in Europe were suffering terrible persecution; I recall my paternal grandmother telling my brother and sisters that the Germans were doing horrible things to the Jews. The year was 1943 and I was six years old.

One day at school while I was in the washroom, another boy entered. His name was John Villar, and he was a year older than I. We began to talk, and during the course of the conversation he asked me if I were Jewish. When I told him that I was, he informed me that "the Jews killed God." Naturally, I was astonished and a bit frightened. I remember going home that day feeling terrible and telling my mother what John Villar had said. I asked her if we had killed God. My mother composed herself as best she could and told me that a long time ago a man lived who said he was God and that, of course, Jews did not believe him. But "others" did, and when he died, the "others" made up the story that the Jews had put him to death because they did not believe a man should call himself God. Later on, she said, the "others" began to worship that man as a god, but Jews worshipped the real God. This answer settled my fears.

Like most American families, we gathered around the living room radio in the evenings. Each December we listened to all the Christmas programs and heard Bing Crosby sing Irving Berlin's "White Christmas." In the streets we saw Santa Clauses making their collections, and every year my father took me down town to see the Macy's holiday window display. My family exchanged presents on Christmas morning and I looked forward to this holiday. Once, I even asked my parents to buy me a Christmas tree, but they said that we were Jewish and Jews did not have Christmas trees in their homes. I watched the world celebrating the great winter festival and it saddened me that I could not participate fully. I knew we had a holiday that occurred approximately the same time, called *Hanukah*, in commemoration of the Jews' ancient victory over the Syrian Greeks. But it seemed pale in comparison with Christmas. *Hanukah* had no pretty carols or radio programs dedicated to it. *Hanukah* had no beautifully decorated trees with cute little animal statuettes beneath them. *Hanukah* had no Santa Claus.

II
A TALE
OF
TWO FAMILIES

I was eight years old when the Second World War ended. In August, 1945, President Truman went on the air and announced to the American people that Japan had surrendered and the war was over. Americans and free people everywhere rejoiced loudly and uninhibitedly. Jews were not able to rejoice with quite as much gusto, however; some five months earlier the world had discovered exactly to what extent and in what manner the Germans had done the "horrible things" to our people that my grandmother had anguished over. Six million Jews had been found guilty of the crime of belonging to the same nation as that man whom the Christians called God.

From kindergarten to my sophomore year in high school, one of my friends was an Italian Roman Catholic named Joseph Rocca. I loved to go to Joe's home at Christmas time; his family seemed happy together, and their holidays were joyous. In contrast, my own home life was not that appealing, at least not for me. My parents' relationship was not what one would call harmonious. My father worked nights and slept during the day, and he hardly spoke to anyone. I remember him as a withdrawn, sullen, uncommunicative person who never once sat down with me for a heart-to-heart talk. My two sisters and brother were teenagers involved with their own social lives and school. My mother never seemed to be finished with housework, and as a child, I never knew the joy of a family worshiping together on the Sabbath or celebrating religious holidays. I thought the Jewish Sabbath and holidays were days of severe restrictions and this did not make them appealing to me.

Joe Rocca's family seemed ideal to me. As devout Christians, they spent their Sundays together in church and after church dined at their "Sabbath" meal table. When I was about ten years old, I was at the Rocca home on a Sunday when they were having ham for dinner. Joe asked me if I would like some. His mother protested that I was not supposed to eat ham because I was Jewish. But no one had ever told ME that, and I said that I would like a sandwich. So Mrs. Rocca gave me my first piece of non-kosher food.

There is a lake in Crotona Park known as the Indian Lake. A man named Berger owned the rowboat concession there, and I used to spend a lot of time at the boat house. I told Mr. Berger one day that I had eaten a ham sandwich and he said I would go to hell for that unless I begged God for forgiveness. Instead of realizing that he was merely having a laugh at the expense of a religiously ignorant ten-year-old, I became very scared. I ran to the nearest synagogue where I earnestly begged God to forgive me for eating forbidden food. That was how I learned that people go to hell for sinning.

III
HEBREW SCHOOL - A BAD EXPERIENCE

At the age of eleven my parents enrolled me in the Hebrew School of Kehilath Israel Synagogue located at 173rd Street and Crotona Park East. There I was taught the Hebrew alphabet, and spent much time simply reading long passages from the prayer book. Except for the *Shema*, the prayer declaring the oneness of God; at no time were the beautiful words of the Jewish liturgy we were reading explained to us. Of course, each of us knew that the Jewish God was one and that our martyrs had died with the *Shema* on their lips. Jewish history was presented to us as a series of tragedies. Occasionally heroes like David or Samson had arisen to save the Jewish people from their enemies; and, of course, there was Judah Maccabee. But most of the time Jews were saved because of leaders like Mordechai or Yochanan ben Zakkai, who used words instead of swords against the gentile leaders. And if God had once, long ago, sent a Moses to Pharaoh, He certainly had not sent one to Hitler.

When I entered TALMUD *TORAH*, Hebrew school, in 1948, Israel had just declared itself an independent and sovereign state. I was still too young to understand much about politics in particular and I knew nothing about the Middle East. The establishment of a Zionist state meant little to me since I had always been told that the Jews would return to Israel when the Messiah came. I did not know that new Samsons, Davids and Judahs were arising who would restore pride to the Jewish people. I did not know that our people had stopped talking through our Mordechais and Ben Zakkais, and had again taken up weapons to help determine our own destiny.

The head teacher at the Kehilath Israel School was completely unsuited to teach young boys. He was a stern, authoritarian figure who seldom smiled and was quick to yell and punish. He exuded no warmth and did not allow himself to have a friendly relationship with any of the students - unfortunately, he was typical of many afternoon Hebrew school pedagogues of that time. He reminded me of my father and we took a personal dislike to one another from the start. For some reason I have never been able to fathom, he felt threatened by me. He thought I needed to be watched very carefully and therefore made me sit at the desk directly in front of his own.

After a full day of classes at the public school, I found Hebrew school a big bore. Like most of the other boys. I would have preferred being out playing ball in the park. My attention often wandered. Many times I ignored what the teacher was saying and tried to engage other students in conversation. The teacher, of course, could not tolerate this, not only because I was disturbing the others, but also because I had the audacity to find his lessons uninteresting.

6

One day, more bored than usual. I decided to create a little diversion in Hebrew class by uttering a Yiddish profanity out loud. The boys roared with laughter, but the teacher, red-faced and fuming, shouted at me to leave and ordered me never to come back. That evening, he called my parents and told them that it would be in the best interest of all concerned to take me out of the school immediately.

I had spent almost a year at Kehilath Israel which was sufficient time to form opinions about Jewish religious teachers. Rabbi Akiva and Maimonides may have been outstanding in their days, but their pedagogic descendants left much to be desired in the eyes of one American twelve-year-old. Incidentally, about a year after I was expelled from that Hebrew school, my teacher was asked to resign. The reason given was that he was not well suited to working with children.

I still had to prepare for my *bar mitsvah* since all Jewish boys are expected to read a section from one of the Books of the Prophets in synagogue when they reach the age of thirteen. My mother brought me to Congregation Nachlat Jacob which was located on Minford Place, not far from the corner of Jennings Street to learn my *haftorah* the reading from the Prophets. I was left each day with a very old man who could not speak English and was in a state of mental and physical deterioration. Many times during my daily hour and a half with him, which seemed like an eternity, he would doze off for long periods. He was unkempt and dirty, and I felt extremely uncomfortable in his presence. Moreover, he did not even begin to teach me my *haftorah* as he was required to do. Whenever he managed to keep awake, he merely had me read more pages of the *siddur*, prayer book, in that incomprehensible Hebrew I was beginning to detest.

I often wondered why I was coming day after day, engaging in exercises in frustration. I knew that my parents were not religious. They wanted me to have "religious instruction" so that I would fulfill my obligation of *bar mitsvah*. Beyond that, I knew they really didn't expect more out of me religiously. I resented them for forcing me to go through this ordeal.

Eventually the men who came to pray at the afternoon service each day began to realize that my new teacher was incapable of preparing me for *bar mitsvah*. Therefore, one of the regular worshipers, a Mr. Benjamin, took over the responsibility of teaching me my *haftorah* This was a relief because now I had someone with whom I could have a rational conversation, Mr. Benjamin lived on Minford Place, and we met in his apartment instead of in the oppressive atmosphere of the synagogue. I also felt more at case with Mr. Benjamin because I knew that he wasn't a rabbi, but nonetheless a knowledgeable Jew. I didn't feel I had to stand in awe of him.

Mr. Benjamin worked with me for several months and on the Sabbath following my thirteenth birthday. I delivered the *haftorah* in the big Minford Place synagogue directly across the street from Mr. Benjamin's small congregation. It was note and letter perfect, but its message was as incomprehensible to me as the *sidaur* had been. I had learned the Hebrew words and melody by rote, but Mr. Benjamin had not explained to me what I was saying. Nor had he even thought of referring me to an English translation. After finishing my *haftorah*, the rabbi of the Minford Place synagogue delivered a congratulatory speech in Yiddish. He expressed the hope that now that I had become a "son of the commandment," I would not lay the *Torah* aside but would carry it with me the rest of my days.

At a *bar mitsvah*, it is customary for the father to make the following public declaration: "Blessed is He who has acquitted me of the burden of religious responsibility for this boy." I do not remember my father making this declaration, and had he done so, it would have seemed strange. Since he had never taken the responsibility of teaching me the Commandments, he could not possibly have acquitted himself of that burden.

I had been given a set of phylacteries several weeks before my *bar mitsvah*. After my *bar mitsvah*, I put them on once or twice, but thereafter laid them aside and did not put them on again. None in my family protested. Besides, no one else in my family used them either. I do not recall what happened to that pair of phylacteries. They disappeared from our home soon after and were not missed. My *bar mitsvah* was for me, as for so many others of my generation, a graduation from *Yidishkeit*, Jewishness.

I had been born a Jew and would die a Jew. That had been taught to me since childhood. Too little time and effort had been devoted to making me fully understand that between birth and death there is life. I did not live as a Jew. I was an American boy in the mid-twentieth century. Judaism, as far as I was concerned, was an old country religion for old men. It was strange, foreign, impotent. It had not saved six million people from death.

IV
PALM SUNDAY
IN THE BRONX

I encountered Jesus again when I was fourteen years old.

The Easter season has always been a difficult time for Jews. It is perhaps the one period of the year that most clearly marks the difference between Jews and Christians. I have always thought the Passion of Jesus to be more emotionally meaningful to Christians than his Resurrection. Indeed, the thought of Jesus' suffering and death has often sent angry mobs in Europe on rampages against the Jews, leading to frenzies of death and destruction. Such events have occurred even within this century. And Jews learned to open the doors of their homes on the first night of Passover to see whether a dead child had been planted on their doorsteps in order to implicate them in the diabolical blood libels, the gentile contention that Jews used the blood of Christian children in their Passover ceremonies.

Palm Sunday, 1951, was a beautiful spring day. Some friends and I decided to go to Bronx Park. While there, we were approached by a group of boys who must have been sixteen or seventeen years old. They were dressed in their Sunday best, and each one wore a palm leaf in the form of a cross on his lapel. Undoubtedly, they had just come from church. I don't know the nature of the sermon they had heard, but they seemed agitated. Obviously, my friends and I were not observing Palm Sunday since we were not dressed up and wore no palms. The group approached us and asked whether we were Jews. Without waiting for our response, they called us "Christ killers" and began to beat us up. It was my first experience with raw Christian anti-Semitism, and I shall never forget it. It was a little taste of what our ancestors had experienced throughout Europe. The lesson sank in. Even here in the United States in the supposedly enlightened twentieth century, we Jews were a defenseless minority at the mercy of gentile animosity.

Not even a decade had passed since the liberation of Auschwitz. Yet here was evidence that the old hatreds were being passed on to the next generation. What had the world learned from the Holocaust?

V
DARK CLOUDS OVER CHARLOTTE STREET

Between the ages of fourteen and sixteen, I felt that I was in a living hell from which there was no escape. In 1952, my father began to exhibit signs of extreme paranoia, and became even more distant from his family. My mother was most affected by him. She and my father began to fight almost daily. He would become vituperative, making wild, preposterous accusations. All communication between him and his children stopped. Only one of my sisters had enough moral stamina to try reconciling my parents, but the attempt was not only futile, it turned my father actively against her also.

Things kept getting worse. If my father were alone in the apartment, for example, he would lock and chain the door, and we would have to bang on it for some time before he would let us in. All our neighbors and friends came to know that something was wrong in our household.

Once, on the eve of *Yom Kippur*, the holiest day in the Jewish calendar, my father came home and, for no apparent reason, suddenly flew into a rage just as we were preparing to retire for the night. He screamed and cursed at my mother and threw furniture around. The scene lasted for only ten minutes but it upset us terribly. There was a severe storm that night, and the lightning and thunder outside added to the violent atmosphere. None of us children said anything; by this time we had decided "not to get involved."

Although we were not observant, I knew that *Yom Kippur* was the most sacred day of the Jewish year, the day, in fact, of reconciliations. My father's choice of the holiest of nights to disturb our peace so viciously imprinted the incident deeply in my memory, and years after he died, my mother and I would sometimes talk about it. I can now understand that he was not fully in control of himself, and that we, his children, share part of the blame for not having tried to confront him, and make him cease his unacceptable behavior. Nevertheless, I do not know if I can ever completely forgive him for what he put us through that night.

The early 1950's were a time of transition for the East Bronx. In a matter of only five years, it had deteriorated into a slum. Jews began to move out as early as 1949, and by 1953 many of our close neighbors had left. Strangers began to move in all around us, which only added to the sense of alienation I was feeling. The area became a dangerous place to live. Many teenagers who were my friends began to join gangs; they saw it as the only way to survive on the streets. Gangs were repugnant to me, and relationships built up over the years disintegrated when my friends became gang members. However, I also had acquaintances who were seriously preparing for college and spent whatever spare time they had on academic work. I had never been encouraged to think about higher education. In most families a child's future is a subject for conversation, but this was not the case in my home. It was simply taken for granted that upon leaving school I would work at whatever job I fell into, and contribute financially to the household. I was totally unprepared for life beyond high school and did not even think about what I would do.

During this period of great isolation, I fell in love for the first time. I was euphoric, walking on clouds, happier than ever before in my life. But as with so many teenage romances, after several months we broke up. and the girl began "going steady" with someone else. The anguish and loneliness that I now felt intensified the hopelessness and despair I had before the relationship had begun. No girl I met after the break-up could measure up to the one who had left me. I soon lost interest in dating and began to get drunk every weekend. Around this same time I developed an anxiety about death. Up to this point in my life I had never thought seriously about dying. Of course, I knew that someday I would pass from this world, but that day had always seemed far away. Now, at sixteen, mortality became a morbid obsession for me. I don't know which doubt assailed me more heavily; either there was no after-life, and I would thus totally cease to exist forever as a thinking personality; or there was an existence to the soul after the body died, in which case my soul might be condemned to eternal damnation. Why I felt enough of a sinner at sixteen to merit damnation, I cannot say. But I brooded about the idea, and it frightened me.

And I had every reason to be fearful. The early 1950s was a disturbing time for Americans in general, and for me in particular. The end of World War Two held out the promise of peace but it was short-lived. Soon a different kind of war arose, the Cold War. Both the United States and Soviet Union now possessed atomic weapons; the possibility of nuclear destruction loomed large. In school we were repeatedly told that an atomic air attack was likely and were given detailed descriptions of its effects. Repeated "take-cover" drills were practiced in the classroom during which we would dive under our desks at a moment's notice to avoid the hypothetical "sudden blinding flash" sure to hit New York in the event of attack. Senator McCarthy was warning that we were in mortal danger from internal enemies, godless communists, who were everywhere and would destroy our freedom and souls. At Morris High School, we were informed in 1953 that graduating seniors would be granted diplomas only if they signed loyalty oaths promising not to engage in subversive activities.

In Korea, young Americans in the prime of life were dying because of the "Cold War." At this time my brother was drafted. The war had reached out and touched my family. On the dark winter's morning my brother left for Ft. Dix, a sense of anxiety and depression overcame me. As a child, I had been taught that only with the coming of the Messiah would war and the ever-impending threat of destruction finally end. He, the Messiah, would bring an era of unending peace to a savage and brutal world. It would be a time when people would "beat their swords into plowshares, and their spears into pruning hooks." Then "nation shall not lift up sword against nation, neither shall they learn war anymore." But until the Messiah were to come, violence and death would remain the way of the world.

VI
ENCOUNTER WITH A CHRISTIAN

I encountered Jesus again - and decisively - when I was sixteen years old.

I had always liked studying languages because they could help me communicate with other peoples. In the eighth grade I began learning French and enjoyed it. I also taught myself Spanish and was able to converse with Puerto Ricans in the neighborhood. Suddenly, I developed an interest in Latin, the parent of the two Romance languages I was studying. I knew that Latin was the liturgical language of the Catholic Church and asked Joe Rocca to help me learn it. By this time, Joe's parents had taken him out of the public school and enrolled him in parochial school. He said that he didn't know Latin except for a few liturgical phrases, and that only priests were expected to master the language. This didn't surprise me, since I was not acquainted with any Jews who could speak Hebrew, and actually believed that only rabbis were supposed to know it.

I was in my senior year at Morris High School. My grades had dropped, and I was barely passing. My average was too low to allow me to matriculate without paying tuition at City College of New York, where many of my schoolmates were headed. I asked my father to pay for my credits on a non-matriculated basis for the first year of college. He refused. He did not want me to go to college and made it clear that he expected me to go to work after high school.

In my homeroom class at Morris High, a boy named Bill Travers sat at the desk directly to my right. Unlike me, Bill had his future all worked out. He knew exactly what he was going to do. Bill Travers was planning to go to seminary when he graduated from high school to become a Baptist minister. In the Morris High School yearbook of the class of 1954, alongside his photo, his stated goal was: "to preach the gospel of Jesus Christ to every living creature." As I sat next to him during that autumn of 1953, I knew nothing about him or his ambitions.

One day I noticed that Bill kept a Bible on his desk. I asked him if the Bible was a bilingual Latin-English one. He turned a sour face to me and asked whether I was Catholic. When I told him that I was Jewish, he immediately relaxed and smiled. He told me that his Bible was a King James edition. I had heard of the King James Bible, of course. It was the Bible out of which the invocations at auditorium assemblies were read. But I had never seen one. At home we had a Hebrew English copy of the Five Books of Moses. Now, for the first time, I had a chance to see the complete scriptures in English.

Bill let me look at his Bible, and I noticed that it contained the "Old Testament" which, I noted, was a translation of the Hebrew books of the Bible, and the New Testament, which contained the Christian books about Jesus. Of course, as a Jew, I had no desire to look at the Christian Scriptures, but I began to thumb curiously through the "Old Testament".

After flipping through many pages, I started scanning the seventh chapter of the book of the prophet Isaiah. Then, I came to the fourteenth verse, the text of which in the King James translation reads as follows:

> Therefore, the Lord Himself shall give you a sign; behold, a virgin shall conceive and bear a child, and shall call his name Immanuel.

I was amazed! A Jewish prophet had predicted that a virgin would give birth to a child. I couldn't believe my eyes.

When I asked Bill about this, he merely nodded his head and smiled. Then he told me that the "Old Testament contained many such prophecies about Jesus, who was the Messiah of Israel. But I argued that Jesus could not have been the Messiah, because we had always been taught that the Messiah would bring lasting peace to the world and make the lion lie down with the lamb."

Yes, Bill agreed, the Messiah certainly would do that; he would do it when he returned to the earth to usher in the Messianic Age, but first he had to come to bring peace to the hearts and souls of individual human beings ready to accept that peace.

"But," I continued arguing, "the Messiah cannot be defeated. He comes to defeat the enemies of Israel."

"Indeed he will," answered Bill assuringly. "Upon his return to earth, when he brings in the kingdom of God, he will overthrow all evildoers and oppressors. As for his being defeated, it was necessary that he die at this first coming in order to save men."

What? What did he mean he had to die to save men? This concept was not only new to me, it was incredible! Bill explained that because Adam and Eve had sinned against God, they had been condemned, not only to death, but to eternal punishment. And not only were Adam and Eve subject to this damnation in hell, but so were all of their descendants - all of us! "But how could that be?" I asked. How could I bear the responsibility for what my earliest ancestors did? I had never encountered such ideas before.

Bill asked me whether I had ever committed a sin in my life. Of course I had, I told him. I supposed that most people commit sins. "No," he said, "not most people - everyone commits sins, and if Adam and Eve had to pay for their sin, why should we be any different from them in God's eyes?"

He quoted Ecclesiastes 7:20:

> For there is not a just man upon the earth that doeth good, and sinneth not.

"But what of our repentance? I asked. "Doesn't God forgive us when we are sorry for our sins and promise not to do them again?"

Bill replied by asking "Have you ever been sorry for any sin you committed?"

"Sure I have," I told him.

"But after having been sorry," he asked, "have you sinned again?"

I had to admit it. "Yes, I had committed sins again." "Well, you see then," he said, "no matter how sorry you are, you will continue to sin. You can't help it. It's part of your nature. We're all sinners." Bill drove the point home. "We have all inherited that original sin from Adam and Eve. And Satan, the devil, has a special interest in continually tempting us to sin. He was the rebel who made Adam and Eve sin, and he wants us to rebel against God as well. Just as Adam and Eve could not withstand him, neither can we."

I still did not understand how one could inherit sins from one's ancestors. This was all new to me. But one thing he said did make sense, and I knew it to be true: people were truly sorry for having sinned, but they went on sinning just the same. Maybe Satan was too powerful to resist. But being sorry wasn't enough. Hell awaited us at the end of our days. Knowingly or unknowingly, Bill had touched upon the fear of death and destruction within me. I could not see my way clear either in this life or the next.

Seeing my discomfort, Bill delivered the coup de grace. "There's nothing to worry about," he assured me. "That's the whole reason God sent His son, the Messiah, into the world. Jesus never sinned, so he was not condemned. Nevertheless, he willingly died as a sacrifice for us so that we would be free of punishment for our sins. All we have to do is open our hearts to him and acknowledge him as our Savior, that is, our Messiah, and we will be saved. We will be saved from hell when we die."

I gasped! Bill was saying that a person could know with certainty beforehand that when he died, he would not go to hell! If only such a thing were really possible, I thought. Bill noticed my silent reaction, and continued preaching to me. He seemed so confident. Never before had I met a teenager with such self-assurance. I marveled at him.

"You know," he continued, "the rabbis want another Temple so they can kill animals and sacrifice them to God for their sins. That's why they tell you that when your Messiah comes, he'll build another Temple for you. But listen, my friend, the Messiah doesn't have to build a Temple for animal sacrifices. His self-sacrifice on the cross is great enough to assure you of forgiveness for your sins. God doesn't want animal sacrifices anyway. He tried that with the Jews originally, but it didn't work. The Jewish people became corrupted through animal sacrifice; they believed God had chosen them above all other peoples, so that they could do anything they wanted and then go to the Temple and kill an animal and get God's favor. Listen to this," he said.

But no one had to tell me to listen. I was all ears, hypnotized. This boy spoke with authority and knowledge! He quickly flipped through the pages of his Bible and read to me:

> Hath the Lord as great delight in burnt offerings and sacrifices as in obeying the voice of the Lord? Behold, to obey is better than sacrifice, and to hearken than the fat of rams.
>
> *1 Samuel 15:22*

> The sacrifices of God are a broken spirit; a broken and contrite heart, O God, thou wilt not despise.
>
> *Psalms 51:17*

To what purpose is the multitude of your sacrifices unto me? saith the Lord. I am full of the burnt offerings of rams and the fat of fed beasts; and I delight not in the blood of bullocks, or of lambs or of he-goats.

Isaiah 1:11

Your burnt offerings are not acceptable, nor your sacrifices sweet unto me.

Jeremiah 6:20

Bill continued reading other similar verses to me. He showed me the book so that I could read them for myself while he said with finality, "Men couldn't make it with God through animals. They abused the system, so God destroyed that corrupt Temple and sent His son as an everlasting sacrifice. You cannot please God anymore with that barbaric practice of killing animals."

I was silent. I didn't know what to say. It was apparent that I couldn't argue with Bill. He knew his Bible and mine. I was ignorant.

The bell rang. We went off to different classes. During and after school that day I just thought about our conversation. I didn't tell anyone about it.

The next day we spoke again. Bill pointed out other "Messianic prophecies" which he claimed were fulfilled by Jesus: that he was to be born in Bethlehem (Micah 5:2); that he was to enter Jerusalem in triumph (Zachariah 9:9); that he was to be crucified (Psalms 22:14-17); and resurrected (Psalms 16:10); and that he was now in heaven waiting to be sent back to earth (Psalms 110:1).

VII
HAS THE
MESSIAH COME?

During the days that followed, Bill and I continued to talk. Of course I had objections, but Bill was able to refute all of them simply and readily. I suppose that inwardly, even from the beginning, I wanted to be convinced. In my world filled with despair and darkness, he was offering me hope and light.

I argued: "But I'm Jewish, and Jesus is for gentiles."

Bill replied: "Jesus is for Christians. Only those who are neither Jewish nor Christians are gentiles. Christians are those who believe in the Messiah, Jesus. Christ is the Greek word for Messiah. Those who accept Jesus as the Messiah become Christians. No one is born a Christian. You become a Christian when you accept Jesus as your personal Savior-Messiah."

"But I don't want to stop being Jewish. I was born a Jew and I want to die a Jew" I argued.

"You don't stop being Jewish when you accept Jesus. You still belong to the Jewish nation," Bill responded. "Jesus was Jewish, and all his disciples and followers were Jewish. The Jews are God's Chosen People. He doesn't want them to disappear. In fact, He promised that they will never disappear. He made an end to other nations, but not to the Jews. In fact, not only do you not stop being Jewish when you accept Jesus Christ, you become a completed Jew! As I said, Jesus was Jewish. 'Jesus' is a Greek name. His Hebrew name was Yeshua."

"But what about all the persecutions Jews have suffered at the hands of Christians?" I asked.

Bill replied indignantly: "Those weren't Christians!

That was the Catholic Church. They used the name of Christ in vain. True Christians never harmed a single Jew. They love and honor God's Chosen People. They wouldn't think of hurting the Jews. After all," Bill added as he turned to Genesis 12:2,3, "God promised Abraham,

> I will make of thee a great nation, and I will
> bless thee, and make thy name great;
> And thou shall be a blessing.
> And I will bless them that bless thee,
> And curse him that curseth thee;
> And in thee shall all the families of the earth be blessed.

"But I can't worship statues and saints," I said.

"Christians don't worship statues and saints," Bill answered. "Only Catholics do that, and they are not real Christians. They haven't accepted Jesus as their personal savior. They claim to be Christians, but they're idolatrous. They worship Mary. We believe that Mary was an ordinary Jewish woman who gave birth to Jesus. She was used by God for that purpose, but she is not to be worshipped."

"But only gentiles, Christians, believe in Jesus," I claimed.

"There have always been Jews who believed in Jesus," Bill replied. "Jesus came to the Jews first. In fact, there are Jews now who believe in him. They're called Hebrew-Christians, and they have their own places of worship."

I was stunned! Did he mean that there were congregations of these Hebrew-Christians? Where were they? Bill promised that he would find out for me where they met. He said he knew of a Jewish girl at Morris High School who was also seeking the Messiah and wanted to know more about the Hebrew-Christians.

"You say that those who don't accept Jesus go to hell. Will all the Jews go to hell then?" I asked.

"We believe that Jesus is coming back to earth soon to set up the Messianic kingdom," Bill replied. "The Jews will accept him just before He returns. God will make sure of that. You can see that prophesied for yourself in the New Testament in Romans, Chapter 11. God needs the Jews. They will be great in the kingdom."

"What of the six million Jews whom Hitler killed?"

Are they all in hell after all that suffering?" I asked. "We believe that most of them saw the light and accepted Jesus just before they entered the gas chambers! Bill answered solemnly. "Can I accept Jesus and return to the synagogue?" I asked.

"You cannot believe that the Messiah has come and then go to the synagogue to pray for the coming of the Messiah."

"What about a good person who doesn't accept him?" I questioned.

"No one can be good without him!" Bill answered.

"And what about those who never heard of him?" I asked.

Bill replied: "That is why we go all over the world preaching about him." Bill replied.

"And what if they don't accept him?" I questioned.

"God is sending us out to preach the gospel of Jesus Christ," Bill responded. 'Gospel' means good news, the good news that all people can gain salvation, not by good deeds, but by inviting the Messiah-Savior into their lives: Whoever hears the gospel preached and rejects it, would be better off never having heard it. God will judge him twice as harshly for having heard it and not accepting it!"

I had run out of arguments. Several weeks had passed since we had begun speaking about Jesus-Yeshua, the Messiah–Savior–Christ. Still, I had told no one else about these conversations. When I left class each day, I went over them in my mind. Bill Travers had spoken to me about God and the Jews in a way no one ever had before. He spoke to my heart. He was genuinely interested in my being saved.

Only years later was I able to analyze fully what he had done. He had exposed my religious ignorance (I did not even know my own Bible). He had touched the Messianic longings in me, longings common to all Israelites. He had offered me the opportunity to "convert" without feeling guilty about being a traitor to my people. He had held out to me a Jewish Jesus with whom I could identify. He had promised to put me in touch with other "saved" Jews who would love, understand, and strengthen me. He had put the "true" Christian people in a new light for me (as allies rather than as enemies). He had played upon and intensified ethnocentric emotions. He had placed me in the same category with sanctified Jewish martyrs. He had recognized my doubts and fears about death and hell, and relieved me of them. He had made me feel, for the first time in my life, that I did not have to do anything to earn God's love; that there was a God in heaven who loved me and gave His love freely. As a sign of this love, He had sent His son into the world to save me! All I had to do was accept. What could be easier?

VIII
COMING TO
ACCEPT JESUS

Accepting Jesus still was not easy for me. Sixteen years of associating the name of Jesus Christ with Jewish suffering held me back from the final commitment. I wanted to believe, but I found it difficult. If Jesus really was the Messiah, we Jews were living lies. The guilt and anxiety produced by these thoughts stuck in my throat. Moreover, assuming Jesus really was the Savior, even if we Jews were chosen of God, we would be damned eternally if we did not accept His son.

Bill had given me a copy of the New Testament and told me to read the Gospels, beginning with John and going on to Matthew, Mark and Luke. The edition he gave me was especially prepared for Jewish readers, he told me, because it contained cross references to "Old Testament" prophecies which Jesus was supposed to have fulfilled,

I began reading the Gospel According to Saint John. Certain verses captured my attention. I underlined and paraphrased them.

Jesus had been sent to the Jewish people who, as a group, did not accept him, but those who did became the children of God. (1:11-12)

Certain Jews did indeed recognize him as the Messiah of Israel. (1:41)

Unfortunately, those who did not accept him aroused God's anger. (3:36)

Moses had given the impossible Law but Jesus offered truth and grace.

However, even Moses had foreseen and prophesied Jesus' coming. (1:17; 5:39, 16, 17)

God had given the Jews a Temple but they had defiled it. Therefore, God had rejected the Temple when He sent His Messiah to be a new Temple. (2:14, 16, 1:21, 221)

God did this because he loved mankind and wanted to save human beings. (3:16)

The rabbis, who were the religious leaders of the people, failed to recognize Jesus as the Messiah. They considered him a threat. Therefore, they chased all Jewish believers in Jesus out of the synagogue. (9:22; 16:2, 3)

But those Jews who accepted him would have their every prayer answered by God and should, therefore, not have to worry about their people's temporary blindness. (14:14)

The problem was that the Jews expected their Messiah to come and set up his kingdom in Israel. They only had to recognize that the world was not the proper place for that kingdom. Jesus the Messiah was too spiritual for the mundane world. His kingdom was in heaven where he waited to receive all of his followers. (18:36)

A reading of the Gospel According to Saint Matthew informed me that:

Jesus had overcome forever the temptation of Satan, the ruler of this world. (4:1-10)

In this world, Jesus would not bring immediate Messianic peace, but rather dissension (10:34) and strife, even among brothers, and between parents and children (10:35), and that one who had compunctions about becoming a follower of Jesus out of fear of parental disapproval, would not merit Jesus' salvation (10.37). Furthermore, the true Christian had to prepare himself and expect to be the object of persecution from friends and strangers alike. Those who could withstand such persecution would win salvation (5:11; 10:22).

Jesus' message was primarily for the Jewish people (5-17; 10:6) but the rabbis, whether out of blindness or spite, have never allowed that message to reach the people of Israel (23:13).

It was now December, and Christmas was approaching. The world around me was rejoicing. "Peace on earth and good will to men." In my home in the east Bronx there was neither peace nor good will. "O little town of Bethlehem...the hopes and fears of all the years are met in thee tonight." There was less and less hope on Charlotte Street, and more and more grief with the passing years. "Noel, Noel, born is the king of Israel." But Israel was not aware that her king had already come.

On Christmas day 1953, I had a conversation with my mother. I told her that I believed that the Messiah we were waiting for might have come already but that we were not aware of it. She asked what I meant, and I explained that perhaps we were looking for the wrong things in a Messiah. We expected a knight on a white horse to ride in and destroy our enemies and establish peace on earth. Might not this concept of God's messenger be too crude? How could peace come to mankind if men's hearts were not at peace? Why should a Messiah destroy our enemies if we were not worthy of him? No Messiah had destroyed the Nazis. Besides, wouldn't it be better and more "spiritual" if, instead of destroying enemies, he turned them into God-fearing friends?

My mother said she didn't have the slightest notion of what I was talking about. I then told her plainly that I believed Jesus to be the Messiah. Perhaps she did not understand fully the implications of what I had said. Perhaps other, more pressing things were preoccupying her. In any case, her reaction to my statement was completely unexpected; instead of becoming angry or, at least, seeming shocked, she merely asked me whether I was serious. When I told her that I was, she simply nodded her head. I now wonder what would have happened if she had objected strongly or expressed outrage. Would it have counterbalanced the proselytizing that was influencing me? Instead, I found no clear response in the person I loved most, the person who had taught me that I was born a Jew and would die a Jew.

Now I realize how deeply I needed my family's love and emotional support at that time, but I was incapable of clearly defining or expressing that need. And they were incapable of understanding it and, perhaps, of fulfilling it even if they had understood it. Certainly, only God was capable of that, and I believed that He was, in fact, doing so by shining a light into my darkness.

IX
A HEBREW AMONG CHRISTIANS

In January of 1954, I returned to school after the winter recess. Bill seemed very happy to see me. He asked whether I had thought further about the gospel over the Christmas holiday, and if I was interested in seeing the power of Jesus at work. I sure was! "Excellent," he said. At the time a local radio station was broadcasting an evangelistic program with a live audience. Bill asked whether I would care to attend one of the broadcasts with him. He said that others who, like me, were searching for God's truth would be there, as well as people who would give testimony about being "saved." Bill added that this testimony, called witnessing might inspire me and help me achieve the faith I needed. I agreed to go.

The studio audience was large and enthusiastic; I was excited about being part of a happy crowd of people who were convinced God loved them and that they were heaven-bound. The smiling and friendly people around us exuded warmth I had never found in any synagogue. To be sure, I had seen Jews rejoice - for example, *on Simchat Torah*, the most spirited of Jewish holidays. But they were rejoicing in the Law, not in each other. And such exuberance was the exception rather than the rule. To me, Jewish religious gatherings were dreary, cold, rigid assemblies of old men, mumbling outlandishly in an unknown language to an incomprehensible God. Somewhere, behind a curtain or up in a balcony, were their old wives. Here it was different. Here there were young people and families together all showing a spontaneous, happy, loving spirit. Here one shouted joyously. Here one held hands and sang hymns to God. Here one felt love!

As the Father hath loved me,
so have I loved you.
Continue ye in my love . . .
These things have I spoken unto you,
that my joy might remain in you,
and that your joy might be full.
This is my commandment,
that ye love one another,
as I have loved you...
Ye have not chosen me,
but I have chosen you...
John 15:9, 11-12, 16

Those words, "Jesus loves me and chose me," may sound corny or trite to some. However, as I sat in that radio studio on that January night alongside my smiling, loving friend Bill, and amid all those smiling, loving Christian men, women and children, those words were electric, and I believed them with all my heart.

Testimonies were given, songs were sung. The program was drawing to a close. The evangelist asked everyone to stand and bow their heads in prayer. He then prayed that the hearts of those who had not yet found their Savior, and hence were still estranged from God, be opened up. He called upon all those who were now ready to accept Jesus as their personal Savior to step forward. I felt Bill watching me. As if by reflex action, I did so, along with about twenty others. We approached the platform where the evangelist was standing. He raised his hands and asked God's blessing upon us lost sheep who had now come into the fold of the righteous.

When the program was over, we were taken to a large room backstage. There we were asked to sign our names to a prayer card saying that we had now accepted Jesus Christ as our personal Savior and were placing our souls and our lives into his loving hands. Bill came into the room and rushed over to shake my hand. He said excitedly, "I just knew you were going to accept him tonight."

Bill then went over to a young man, one of the evangelist's assistants, and whispered something to him. The young man's face broke out into a broad smile. He announced to the others present, "Mr. Sherman is a Hebrew!" Shouts of "Amen!" and "Praise the Lord!" echoed around the room. My being called a Hebrew should have been a clue to me. Now that I had accepted Jesus, these Christians would no longer refer to me as a Jew.

X
FAMILY REACTIONS

I spent the next few days in anxiety. How would I break the news of my salvation to my family? I was living at home so it would be difficult to hide. And anyway, why should I want to hide it?

He that loveth father or mother more than me is not worthy of me. He that taketh not his cross, and followeth after me, is not worthy of me.

Matthew 10:37, 38

Whosoever therefore shall confess me before men, him will I confess also before my Father which is in heaven. Think not that I am come to send peace on earth. I came not to send peace, but a sword. For I am come to set a man at variance against his father, and the daughter against her mother, and the daughter-in-law against her mother-in-law. And a man's foes shall be they of his own household.

Matthew 10:32-36

And so I confessed my Messiah Jesus before the members of my family. I expected either of two reactions. On the one hand, they would try to reason with me or at least refer me to others who could show me the gravity of what I had done. Or they would drive me out and sit shiva, as if in mourning for me, which is historically what the Jewish community has done to Jewish converts to Christianity. But my family was capable of neither reaction. My mother was pained, but immobilized, my sisters vehement but ineffective, and my brother uninvolved but "satisfied" that I had "found religion." And my father's reaction; when he saw me reading my New Testament, he yelled at me, "Get rid of that! I don't want that damn book in this house!" But while he didn't want it in our home, he did nothing to get rid of it! Suddenly it dawned on me; I could accept Jesus if I wanted, and my family would do nothing about it. They didn't like my decision, of course, but they lacked the will to do anything about it. Clearly, at sixteen I possessed more religious strength than all of them put together.

I was now convinced that God was on my side and I was the only complete Jew among them. None of them knew the strength of the Messiah Yeshua except me, and I hoped to be his messenger to them, and, by his strength, bring us all together as a happy family in God. The only non-Jews I told about my conversion were the Roccas. I thought they would be sympathetic, but they were not. Joe's mother was concerned that my family might hold them responsible in some way for my conversion. Joe himself said that belief in Jesus was not enough to make me a Christian; I would have to join a church, in particular, the Roman Catholic Church. He also told me that just as I had denied Moses, so one day would I deny Jesus. I left his house in anger and never discussed religion with him again.

Part II

The people gathered themselves unto Aaron, and said unto him, "Come on, make us gods which shall go before us; as for this Moses, the man that brought us up out of the land of Egypt, we know not what is become of him..." and they said, "These be thy gods, O Israel, which brought thee up out of the land of Egypt."

Exodus 32:1,4

The simple son asks: What is this?

Passover Haggadah

XI

THE HOUSE OF THE PRINCE OF PEACE

Beth Sar Shalom, the House of the Prince of Peace, was a Hebrew-Christian mission on West 72nd Street in Manhattan. It was operated by the American Board of Missions to the Jews, a Chicago-based organization in existence since the turn of the century, and was the main center on the East Coast directed at proselytizing Jews.

The mission was founded by Leopold Cohn, who, born in Beresin, Hungary, called himself "rabbi". Cohn believed the Messiah had come in the person of Jesus. In the late 1880s, he opened a mission in the Brownsville section of Brooklyn. It prospered as a result of support from prominent Protestant evangelical groups. In 1924, he and his son Joseph established the American Board of Missions to the Jews in the Williamsburg section of Brooklyn, and in 1945, they acquired a building on West 72nd Street in Manhattan, and gave it the impressive name *Beth Sar Shalom*.

It was from this mission that the so-called Jews for Jesus movement split off in the early 1970s. Although the Manhattan based *Beth Sar Shalom* is no longer functioning, the American Board of Missions to the Jews operates several missions with similar objectives in the Greater New York Metropolitan area and across the country.

The *Beth Sar Shalom* building on West 72nd Street contained a library and offices on the upper floors, and a meeting hall or auditorium on the main floor. The hall was designed to seat about 200 people although I never saw more than 40 or 50 people there at one time. Structurally, it resembled a simple Protestant church with rows of pews and a pulpit on a raised platform up in front. The rear of the room and the vestibule just outside contained racks and tables displaying a number of tracts "proving" that Jesus is the Messiah promised to Israel.

Bill Travers led me to *Beth Sar Shalom*. It was the Hebrew Christian congregation he had referred to when he told me that one could be Jewish and Christian at the same time. I went there each Sunday afternoon to attend services and study the Bible. From the very first time I entered *Beth Sar Shalom*, I learned what acceptance into a religious group means. I was showered with attention and welcomed as a lost son coming home. The people seemed eager to make me feel welcome and to teach me about the true "biblical" Jewish service of God. Not only would I learn the meaning of Jesus' love, but perhaps more important, I would learn how to witness to my fellow Jews in order that they also might ultimately be saved.

Of course, the prospect of witnessing to my family was beautiful.

One example of the acceptance I received there had to do with appearance. On weekends I used to dress casually, usually in jeans. At no time was I told that I had to dress up to attend services. This was so unlike the demands made of people in synagogues I had attended. I did not have to "look right" for people if I looked all right to God and to Jesus. One day, after I had been going to *Beth Sar Shalom* for a few months, one of the sisters, as the female worshippers were called, took me aside and told me that if I needed clothing, she would see to it that I got whatever I wanted. I had only to ask. She said that I was not to interpret this offer as a suggestion that I was improperly dressed, but simply to understand that my fellows in Christ cared about me.

The people at *Beth Sar Shalom* were very interested in knowing how my family was reacting to my confessing Jesus as the Messiah. I told them that they were not happy about it but were doing nothing to hinder me in my newfound faith. However, this was not enough for me. I wanted to know what I could do to help my family understand that the Messiah had already come and that they could achieve unity and happiness if they would only turn to God and lay their burdens at his feet. I was encouraged to witness to them, and to my friends, by showing how Jesus had fulfilled "Old Testament" prophecies, and, of course, to pray for them. Others at the *Beth Sar Shalom* would also be praying for them.

I recall reading the following verses from the King James Bible to my mother and asking her to tell me which Testament they were from:

> His visage was so marred more than any man,
> And his form more than the sons of men;...
> Who hath believed our report?
> And to whom is the arm of the Lord revealed?
> He is despised and rejected of men;
> A man of sorrows, and acquainted with grief:
> And we hid as it were our faces from him;
> He was despised and we esteemed him not.
> Surely he hath borne our griefs.
> And carried our sorrows...
> He was wounded for our transgressions,
> He was bruised for our iniquities:
> And with his stripes we are healed.
> All we like sheep have gone astray;
> We have turned every one to his own way;
> And the Lord hath laid on him the iniquity of us all.
> He is brought as a lamb to the slaughter,
> And as a sheep before his shearers is dumb,
> So he openeth not his mouth.
> For the transgression of my people was he stricken?
> Because he had done no violence,
> Neither was any deceit in his mouth.
> Yet it pleased the Lord to bruise him;.

For he shall bear their iniquities …
Because he hath poured out his soul unto death:
And he was numbered with the transgressors;
And he bare the sin of many,
And made intercession for the transgressors.

Isaiah 52:14-53:12

I knew she would say they were from the New Testament, and, of course, she did. She, as well as virtually every other Jew I knew, was ignorant of the Bible. What better proof could there be that our Messiah had to suffer for our sins so that we would be free of them? Jews could pray and cry on *Yom Kippur* all they wished; without the "blood sacrifice" demanded by God, their sins would remain. However, those to whom I preached remained impervious to "prophecies" and other biblical texts I offered as proof. They did not argue with them; they simply ignored or ridiculed them. So much for using texts as proof.

I spoke about Jewish destiny and how Jesus the Messiah completes our choosiness. We had been chosen as a people, but when Israel recognized her king, we would be chosen in faith as well. When I preached to those close to me, they told me that Jews do not have to be "completed"-they are born complete-and that Israel would only recognize a king who would bring everlasting peace to the world. The idea of a Messiah who dies to save men's souls was ludicrous to them.

I brought home tracts explaining the gospel message to Israel. The tracts wound up in the garbage.

One day my older sister asked me, "Do you really believe that *zeyde,* grandfather, and *bobe,* grandmother, are in hell?"

I stopped witnessing to my family.

I was the real Jew, the "biblical" Jew. The rabbis had kept my family in ignorance just as they had kept the rest of Israel from seeing God's truth. The Bible said that only a remnant of faithful Israel would be saved. I was part of that remnant. If other Jews refused to see that, "let their blood be on their heads."

Matthew 27:25

XII
BECOMING A
"COMPLETE JEW"

The services at *Beth Sar Shalom* consisted of hymn singing, discussion of biblical passages by the mission leaders, a sermon or personal testimony, and a final prayer addressed to the God of Abraham, Isaac, and Jacob, in the name of His son, Jesus the Messiah. Unlike subsequent Hebrew-Christian groups, such as Jews for Jesus, which have come up with original "Jewish-sounding" songs, the hymns I heard at *Beth Sar Shalom* were standard Protestant ones.

The biblical discussions usually tried to reveal the "true" meaning of Judaism, and to prove, through Old Testament' texts, that Jesus was the Messiah. They were mainly based on tracts published by the American Board of Missions to the Jews (some of these tracts are still in circulation today).

The tract, *We have Found the Messiah,* informed us that "there are 456 references in the 'Old Testament' to the Messiah," and that the prophets "foretold the coming of a new religion." It also states that the Messiah "would come during the time of the Second Temple."

Why did the Messiah have to die? elaborated on the theme of the saving death of Jesus.

Can a Jew Become a Follower of Jesus Christ and Remain a Jew? assured us that Hebrew-Christians are the true Israelites, but that traditional Jews have allowed the Talmud of the rabbis to replace the Bible and thus have obscured the way to belief in God. As proof of this, the tract pointed to the growing secularization of American Jewry. It neglected to say that secularization was taking place among gentiles in the United States as well.

Personal testimony by members consisted of the accounts of their having found Jesus, and how he changed their lives.

About the fourth week that I was at *Beth Sar Shalom*, I was called upon to give testimony. I got up and spoke: "Friends, St. Paul informs us in his Letter To The Hebrews that 'God, who at sundry times and in divers manners spoke in times past unto the fathers through the prophets, hath in these last days spoken to us through His son, whom He hath appointed heir of all things.' (1:1-2) Surely these must be the last days since Jesus our Messiah prophesied that we would hear of wars, famines, sicknesses, earthquakes, persecutions. What better description of our age than this? All around us we see unhappiness and the world given over to Satan. As to God speaking to us through His son, I must say that Jesus personally spoke to me as an inner voice and revealed to me that he is really God's son for whom our people have been waiting for thousands of years. Since I accepted him I no longer fear anything in this world or the next."

I sat down. "Amen's" and "Hallelujahs" rang out. I loved hearing these outbursts of praise to the Lord. It was a spontaneous demonstration of the love of God; I had never heard anything like that in a synagogue, and it thrilled me.

One Sunday evening I was coming home from a *Beth Sar Shalom* meeting and as I was leaving the subway, Holy Bible in hand, I met my social studies teacher, Mr. Shuster. He asked what I was reading, and when I showed him, he smiled and asked which religious organization I was involved with. As I told him about *Beth Sar Shalom*, he gave me a concerned look and asked how I got along with my father.

I was angry at the implication that bad relationships at home had led me to seek God through Jesus, and I told him so. Had not Jesus himself spoken to me in my heart? Had not the plain truth of the Messiah's coming been revealed to me through God's own words, the very same Holy Bible I held in my hand?

Mr. Shuster was very kind. He apologized for having antagonized me and said he had no intention of offending me or of making light of my religious quest. He merely wanted to know, he explained, about the religious state of my family, since it seemed strange to him for a Jewish boy to be a professing Christian.

I told him that by becoming a Christian I was now a "completed" Jew. Mr. Shuster looked pained. "Am I incomplete then?" he asked.

I felt uneasy witnessing to him. I did not want to offend him; after all, he was an authority figure whom I had to see every day in social studies class. I was speechless.

Seeing my discomfort, he said, "Perhaps we can talk tomorrow after class."

The suggestion excited me. Here was a fellow Jew who knew I had accepted Jesus and yet was not hostile toward me; indeed, he was friendly. Was something inside me, this time not of Jesus but of the *pintele yid,* the Jewish spark, responding to a hope of genuine Jewish fellowship? I know only that I see the same reaction today in young Jewish men and women influenced by proselytizers who tell me they believe their Messiah has come. They too seem to long for the company of traditional Jews who will take the time to speak to them of the Jewish God. They are hungry for the interest and concern of fellow Jews who will relate to them as Jews. They have experienced so little of it.

The next day after class I eagerly approached Mr. Shuster and asked what he had to say to me. To my surprise, he seemed embarrassed and flustered. He said that he really had nothing to add to our conversation of the previous day, except that I should think carefully about my new commitment. I was more than disappointed; I was crestfallen. Apparently Mr. Shuster had a failure of nerve or else had decided that the Board of Education might not approve of a teacher's interfering with a student's religious preference. Once again, I felt, that traditional Jews had nothing of value to tell me about religion.

XIII
A PASSOVER
IN
EAST NEW YORK

Leopold Cohn's son, Joseph, wrote a tract entitled *The Broken Matzoh*, in which he explained that the three Passover matsot, unleavened breads, represented the Father, Son, and Holy Ghost of the Trinity, and that the middle *matzoh*, Jesus, had been broken on the cross for all time. He was our paschal sacrifice; indeed, he had chosen Passover as the time for his very own death in order that his saving blood might appear symbolically on the doorposts of believers' hearts, saving them from Satan, the angel of death.

The Sunday before Passover in 1954, we reenacted the Last Supper of Jesus Christ at the *Beth Sar Shalom*. We were given wine and *matzoh*. One of the "brothers" said that this was a special *kiddush,* benediction, in honor of Jesus, the wine being his blood, the *matzoh*, his body.

> Verily, verily, I say unto you, except ye eat the flesh of the Son of man, and drink his blood; ye have no life in you. Who so eateth my flesh, and drinketh my blood hath eternal life; and I will raise him up at the last day. For my flesh is meat indeed; and my blood is drink indeed. He that eateth my flesh, and drinketh my blood, dwelleth in me, and I in him. As the living Father hath sent me, and I live by the Father: so he that eateth me; even he shall live by me. This is the bread which came down from heaven: Not as your fathers did eat manna, and are dead: He that eateth of this bread shall live forever.
>
> *John 6:53-58*

My mother's side of the family lived in Brooklyn. Each year we would go to the East New York section of Brooklyn for the first *seder*, the opening Passover meal. My mother's brothers would *pravet,* conduct, the *seder*, and over fifty relatives would be present. It was a wonderful family get-together, and I always looked forward to it. This year in particular, because my "Jewish consciousness" had been raised, I especially anticipated the happy feeling of participating in the festival of freedom. Of course, the "true" (i.e., Christological) significance of each ritual would add to my participation and enjoyment.

I spoke about redemption with members of my family during the meal. I told them how grateful we ought to be for all the miracles that God had done for our fathers and for us. One of my cousins said that he did not believe in God at all, but he thought that people needed religion to hold them together and to make them feel that Someone was taking care of them. Soon others joined in and agreed with him. I was appalled! If they were representative of misguided Jews, and did not even believe in traditional Judaism, how could I expect them to see the "completed" Judaism of the Bible? The more I thought about the incident, the more disgusted I became. It ruined whatever enjoyment I had for my family's celebration of the *seder*. Furthermore, it made me aware of the growing secularization of the Jewish people. Because they were not anchored in Jesus, I felt Jews were drifting further and further away from God's salvation. The Jewish people's only hope was a dramatic Divine revelation. I was convinced that this was imminent. After all, God had promised that His Chosen People would be saved; He would perform a miracle, if nothing else worked, to accomplish this.

XIV
A DENT
IN
MY NEW FAITH

Our "sisters" and "brothers" often told us that it was our duty to witness Jesus to others, but that we would be persecuted by the world for this witness. Those of us who said we were not being persecuted unduly for our newly found Messiah were advised that perhaps we were not witnessing enough.

What, I wondered, did they want us to do? Each of us had come to Jesus, I supposed, to be free of suffering. As it says in Matthew (11:28-30),

Come to me all ye that labor and are heavy laden, and I will give you rest. Take my yoke upon you, and learn of me; for I am meek and lowly in heart; and ye shall find rest unto your souls. For my yoke is easy; and my burden is light.

I had seen street corner preachers who witnessed for Jesus. One was a woman named Rosie who used to put up an American flag in the Times Square area on Saturday nights and scream damnation at passersby. This was not my image of someone who had received the peace of Christ. Did they intend us to emulate this insanity? I refused to make a spectacle of myself and my faith in that distasteful manner. And besides, people like Rosie always seemed so *goyish*, alien, to me with that crass type of appeal. I never could fully accept threatening people with hell's fire to induce them to accept my Jewish Messiah. Besides, my mission was not to the gentiles, but to "the lost sheep of Israel." (Matthew 10:5,6)

Actually, I did very little witnessing at all; God had revealed-His Messiah to me, and I was confident that He would do so to others in His own time. However, one day in the early summer of 1954, I unexpectedly got an opportunity to witness to Jews. It was to be one of the first dents in my "Messianic" faith.

When the weather was warm, I would spend my after-school hours at a playground in Crotona Park. One afternoon I was sitting on a bench with a friend. Nearby was a group of Orthodox Jewish students. At first I was not aware of them, for I was engrossed in a conversation with my friend about biblical prophecy concerning the Messiah. The yeshiva boys overheard part of the conversation and became incensed at hearing a Jew proclaim Jesus as the Messiah. Before I knew it, they were standing around me, angrily shouting me down. No, they insisted, the so-called Messianic prophecies preached by Christianity were nothing of the sort. They were old arguments, they said, which had already been refuted by the great Jewish religious teachers of the Middle Ages.

"But," I stuttered, "doesn't Isaiah in his fifty-third chapter say that Jesus would be the suffering Messiah?"

They sneered. According to them, Isaiah 53 wasn't about Jesus at all, but symbolically describes the Jewish people as the suffering servants of God.

"What about Isaiah 7:14?" I asked. "Doesn't it say that a virgin will give birth to a divine son?"

They laughed in a condescending manner. "That's what the *goyim* say." Then one student challenged me. "You show us where Isaiah talks about a virgin birth, and don't show us any *goyishe*, missionary English Bible. The Hebrew doesn't say 'virgin' at all; it says "young woman." And if you read the entire chapter you will see that it has nothing at all to do with the Messiah, much less with that *mamzer*, Jesus of Nazareth."

The students waved in disgust and walked away. Suddenly one of them turned back and yelled at me. "Hey you, *meshumad!* You know what we say about that *mamzer? YESHU! Yod-Shin-Vav, (Y-S-V) Yimakh Shemo Vzichrono!*" Years later, I learned that the Hebrew phrase means, "May his name and memory his blotted out!"

Had they been a little kinder, I might have run after them, spoken to them, found out then and there what it would take me almost a decade and a half to discover, i.e., that I was already "saved" when I was born. There had been no need to turn to Jesus for salvation. The Jewish people, since their encounter with God at Sinai, had maintained a relationship of saving grace with Him without need of any other savior. One had only to look at that same book of Isaiah (43:11, 45:21, 60:16) to appreciate this.

But this was not yet the age of religious outreach. The Jewish community had yet to feel the loss of thousands of its young to Jesus and to the cults. To those yeshiva boys I was a *meshumad,* a traitor or apostate. I had gone over to the "other side." This encounter taught me something, however. I now realized that there were Jews who knew the Bible, not only the *Torah,* the five books of Moses, but the Prophets as well. If their interpretation of these prophets differed from that of Hebrew-Christianity, then it must be a manifestation of their blindness or rabbinical misdirection that Christians had warned me about. I comforted myself with these thoughts, but the realization that there was a different traditional Jewish interpretation of Isaiah, and presumably of the other prophets, stuck with me.

XV
JESUS:
MESSIAH OR GOD?

Christianity teaches that God is composed of a Trinity, ie., three persons: the Father, usually identified as the God of the "Old Testament," the Son, Jesus; and the Holy Spirit, the invisible Divine presence in the world. Each of these three beings is co-equal, so that any one of them can be referred to as God. Therefore, Jesus himself, in Christian dogma, is not only God's physical son, he is God Himself.

Consequently, a Jew (indeed, anyone) who converts to Christianity is expected to accept the doctrine of the Trinity, and hence that Christ is God. The convert who hesitates to do so may well encounter death while in a state of sin as reference to *John 8:24* points out, where Jesus says, "I said therefore unto you, that ye shall die in your sins, for if ye believe not that I am He, ye shall die in your sins."

In fact, the missionaries to Jews have gone so far as to reinterpret the basic concept of Judaism, the *Shema*, "Hear O Israel, the Lord is our God, the Lord is one" *(Deuteronomy 6:4)* so as to support the idea of the Trinity: They claim that the Hebrew word echad means, not "one" but "unity", and that the threefold use of the Divine name, "the Lord.. Our God, the Lord..." indicates the oneness of God to be a tri-unity.

When Christian missionaries approach gentiles, they have no qualms about initially preaching the divinity of Jesus. However, when they are witnessing to Jews, they present the Messianic aspect of Jesus first, thereby appealing to the Messianic longings of the Jew. Perhaps they fear that telling a Jew "up front" that Jesus is God will turn him off since the oneness of the Deity is so indelibly imprinted on the Jewish psyche. Every Jew knows that Jewish martyrs died with the *Shema*, the prayer proclaiming the oneness of God, on their lips, denying the Church's attempt to force a profession of the Trinity upon them.

Eventually, however, the Hebrew-Christian is expected to embrace Christian dogma in its entirety. Here I had a great deal of difficulty. I had been brought up with the traditional Jewish view that God would send a Messiah. I had never been told that God himself would be the Messiah in the form of a man. The Jewish abhorrence of the idea of corporealness of the Deity made me instinctively resist the doctrine of the Incarnation of God in human form. Yes, I could accept that Jesus was His physical son; in a sense, we are all physical sons of God. Even one of the Gospels had stated as much (John 1:12). But that God should become incarnate in the form of a human being, no, emphatically not!

And He said (to Moses), thou canst not see my face, for no man shall see Me, and live.
Exodus 33:20

In the Crotona Park playground I met a man named Arnie Greenberg during the early autumn of 1954. He was a Jehovah's Witness. Here was a Jew who believed in Jesus as the son of God but whose religious sect denied the Trinity. "Show me a verse in scripture that talks about Jesus being God," he said. "I challenge anyone to do that."

I pointed out that in John 1:1, it says, "In the beginning was the Word (Jesus), and the Word was with God, and the Word was God." Arnie Greenberg replied: "The Greek text doesn't say that at all. It says, and the Word was divine.'"

I continued. In John 10:30, it says, "I and my Father are one.

Arnie Greenberg replied: "Jesus and God are of one accord. Any person who follows God's word can say that he and God are one. According to John 14:28, Jesus also said, 'My Father is greater than I.'" I then noted that in Colossians 1:15, it says "Jesus) who is the image of the invisible God." Arnie Greenberg replied: "All human beings are the image of God."

So there were Christians who did not believe Jesus was God. What a revelation! This was more like it. I had many conversations with Arnie, and several times I attended Sunday services with him at the Jehovah's Witness Kingdom Hall. But after several weeks, it became apparent that the Jehovah's Witnesses had nothing to offer me. True, they called God by the transliteration of the Hebrew Tetragrammaton, J-H V-H, but that's as far as they went. They denied being Jews and claimed that the status of Chosen People had passed from Jews to Christians. In fact, they said Jews as a people were doomed for having rejected Jesus as the Christ. Besides, their religion appeared to me to be drab: no holidays, no symbols, no rituals. I considered them to be unpatriotic because they refused to salute the flag of the country that protected them. And when it came to medicine, they appeared to be just plain crazy, refusing blood transfusions even when their lives and those of their children depended on it!

No. I was a *Hebrew-Christian,* chosen of the chosen. I could not yet accept Jesus as God, but I continued to meditate and pray for guidance.

XVI
A CHRISTIAN WITHOUT A CHURCH

In June, 1954, I graduated from Morris High, and on graduation day, Bill Travers said to me, "Hold fast to Jesus and don't let anything or anyone causes you to deny him. If you ever do give him up," he warned, "you will give up everything. You'll give up being Jewish too, everything. I've seen it happen to others."

That was the last time I heard from him until December of that year when he called to wish me a Merry Christmas and to see how I was doing. Was I still strong in the Lord? Yes. Was I still at *Beth Sar Shalom*? Yes. But what was I doing with my life? About a year had passed since I had accepted Jesus. It was now time for me to join a church and be baptized. There, I would meet other young people, my social peers in Jesus.

I was stunned! What was he saying? Baptized? Me? What need had I to be baptized? Baptism was for gentiles! They had to be baptized in order to cleanse themselves of their paganism when they accepted our God. I was already one of God's chosen - chosen in nation and in religion. Of course, I did not say this to Bill. I didn't want to hurt his feelings. He had helped to direct me to my Messiah, but after all, he was only a gentile. We Hebrew-Christians all realized that in the coming kingdom we would be first.

To be sure, the gentiles had acknowledged Jesus before we had, and in greater numbers, but that had been God's plan as revealed by St. Paul in the eleventh chapter of the Epistle to the Romans. The New Testament made it clear that the gentiles were only second choice. Jesus had come "to the Jew first" (Romans 1:16). And why would I want to leave *Beth Sar Shalom* to join a church and isolate myself from my fellow Hebrews? Church was for *goyim*, gentiles.

What Bill had said about social peers touched a chord in me, and was more to the point. The people at *Beth Sar Shalom* were kind to me, but they were mostly older, lonely people, and some of them were not even Jewish according to Jewish law. I had little in common with them as individuals. For all the love they showed me, I was never invited to any of their homes. At a church I probably would find people my own age with whom I could become friendly. (Since the time of my involvement, Hebrew-Christianity, via Jews for Jesus and similar groups, has changed. It has become part of the "youth culture" for many young Jews who give each other emotional support.)

Speaking to Bill on the phone reminded me of an incident several weeks earlier. I had gone down to the *Beth Sar Shalom* one Sunday, and, as I entered, I saw a girl who looked about eighteen years old. She was reading a tract in the back of the room. My heart melts as I approached her and engaged her in the conversation. Here was someone my own age!

Her appealing smile and southern accent captivated me and said she was visiting relatives in the neighborhood in passing had noticed the mission. Her curiosity had brought her in. Was she Jewish? "Oh no!", she exclaimed. My excitement dimmed.

I started to sense, and my conversation with Bill reinforced the thought, that no Jewish girl would have me once my profession of faith became known. The only viable relationships I would probably have would be with a shiksa, non-Jewish women. The realization was a shock to me! In recent years I have spoken to many Hebrew-Christians, and this has been corroborated. I have never met a married Hebrew-Christian who did not wind up with a gentile mate.

XVII
A CHRISTIAN VIEW OF HELL

Christianity postulates that Jesus saves souls from eternal damnation in hell. This hell is ruled by the devil who is called Satan. It is Satan who caused man to sin originally and who continues to tempt man.

Christianity has given so much importance to Satan that it has actually elevated him to the position of world ruler, a kind of god-opposite-to-God. As a result, it has bequeathed a grim legacy to all of Christendom. The fruits of this legacy have been witch-hunts and inquisitions that have at times created a hell-on-earth.

The "reward" of sin is torture in hell for those who do not have Christ's saving grace. As Bill pointed out to me, "works", i.e., good deeds, count for nothing in themselves. Man's hope that he can justify himself before God has been denounced as sinful pride by Christians from the time of Jesus to present day evangelical preachers. And all of these Christians have leaned on Biblical support, to wit:

> How then can man be justified with God?
> Or how can he be clean that is born of A woman?
> Yea, the stars are not pure in His sight.
> How much less man, that is a worm?
> *Job 25:4-6*

Fear of hell is quintessential to the Christian missionary message, and, as I stated, it helped motivate me to accept Jesus as Savior.

And yet life itself is harsh and cruel. This very world can itself be a place of torment and damnation. Yes, "The imagination of man's heart is evil from his youth" (Genesis 8:21), and justice requires that the sins of a human being be requited "measure for measure." But should the good that he does in this world be ignored in the next one?

As I wrestled with the doctrine of the Trinity on one side and asked for guidance from above, I grappled with the problem of sin and hell on the other side. Of course, Jesus had saved me from hell. But I was a sinner. Otherwise, why should I have been afraid of hell? But how could those who died in infancy, for example, be condemned to hell's fire by a just God? Or my saintly grandparents? Or six million innocents murdered by the followers of my Messiah? Hadn't Abraham our father already stood up at the beginning of our history and confronted the Almighty about this very issue?

> Wilt Thou also destroy the righteous with the wicked? That be far from Thee to do after this manner, to slay the righteous with the wicked, and that the righteous should be as the wicked; that be far from Thee! *Shall not the Judge of all the earth do justly?*
>
> *Genesis 18:23, 25*

I had to ask someone for a "second opinion," and the only one I knew to consult was Arnie Greenberg. "There's no such thing as hell's fire and eternal suffering," he affirmed with indignation. "So-called Christians show their real lack of compassion by even dreaming up such concepts."

"But doesn't Scripture itself talk about hell? And didn't Jesus come to save us from hell?" I asked

His answer was decisive. "Jesus was sent to save us from death!"

"But everyone dies!" I protested.

"Yes," he explained. "And Jesus himself died. But he rose from the grave, and all who put their trust in him will rise from the grave on the final day. I read in Scripture that Jesus was placed in the grave, but there is nothing in the Bible about him going to hell. The story of 'The Harrowing' is a Roman Catholic myth!" (The Harrowing of Hell is the Catholic's term to describe the descent of Jesus into hell at his death in order to rescue the souls of the righteous who had died prior to his appearance on earth.) "But the Bible mentions hell," I responded.

"Yes," he said. "Most Bibles translate the Hebrew words *sheol* and *gehenna,* and the Greek word *hades,* as 'hell' but let's look more closely at what the real meaning of hell is." Then he referred to four texts:

> And fear not them which kill the body, but are not able to kill the soul; but rather fear him which is able to destroy both soul and body in hell.
>
> *Matthew 10:28*

> ... of the resurrection of Christ, that his soul was not left in hell, neither his flesh did see corruption.
>
> *Acts 2:31*

> For the wages of sin is death; but the gift of God is eternal life through Jesus Christ our Lord.
>
> *Romans 6:23*

> ...and death and hell delivered up the dead who were in them... and death and hell were cast into the lake of fire.
>
> *Revelation 20:13, 14*

Arnie analyzed them as follows: "First of all, notice that the soul, whatever that is, is destroyed in hell along with the body. It is destroyed, not tormented. Second, Christ's soul, the Hebrew word nefesh means 'life' or 'self'; he himself was not left in hell, nor did his body decompose. Third, the penalty for sin is death, not torture. And last, at a future time, both death and hell are to be consumed in a place of fire. If hell were a place of fire, how could fire destroy it? It is obvious from these contexts that what is commonly called hell is, in reality, the grave. That is, those who die without salvation are obliterated, not tortured. They do not rise at the final resurrection to eternal life. Death, not torture, is their penalty. The just Lord would not torture souls for eternity. He is not a sadist."

So Arnie laid it out for me. People did not roast in hell eternally. Arnie's Jehovah's Witness theology concerning the afterlife was one degree more acceptable than that of Hebrew-Christianity, i.e., that of classical Christianity, but it was only one degree more acceptable. It did away with eternal torment for those outside Christ's grace, but it still included righteous unbelievers among the unsaved. Instead of roasting them forever, it consigned them to extinction for mere unbelief! They were still damned and removed from God through their rejection of Jesus. Arnie had not solved the problems of hell and the grave to my complete satisfaction.

XVIII
CHRISTIAN
ANTI-SEMITES

By the spring of 1955, I had been a Hebrew Christian for almost a year and a half, and certain questions had still not been answered to my satisfaction. My fellow believers in Jesus might have said that my basic problem was that I questioned at all. I had accepted Jesus as my Messiah and Savior. Why did I not rest now and let him guide my life? Why didn't I simply trust him? Why, after having been saved, was I still agitated?

They might have said these things to me if I had shared my doubts with them. But I did not. It was not that I was worried about confiding in them. That's what Christian fellowship is supposed to be about. You are my brother in Christ. We all have doubts at one time or another. Doubt is Satan's work. Let us, therefore, strengthen one another. No, fear of sharing my doubts was not the issue. It was simply that these people seemed to be so completely satisfied and at ease in their faith that I had no wish to disturb them. Better to keep still than do Satan's work. Better to "stand in awe, and sin not; commune with your own heart upon your bed, and be still." (Psalms 4:4)

> I remembered God, and was troubled:
> I complained, and my spirit was overwhelmed.
> Selah.
> Thou holdest mine eyes waking:
> I am so troubled that I cannot speak.
> I have considered the days of old, the years of ancient times.
> I call to remembrance my song in the night.
> I commune with mine own heart:
> And my spirit made diligent search.
> *Psalms 77:3-6*

Whether or not I could have worked these difficulties out is moot. A new problem arose which made the other ones seem petty. The problem was grave and completely diverted my attention from theological concerns.

One Sunday afternoon, I entered the *Beth Sar Shalom* and found a group of "brothers" and "sisters" at the back of the chapel. They were listening to someone in their midst delivering a harangue. The man was angry, and his temper made his red face even redder. A large vein stood out on his neck as he spoke bitterly. "You can't work with these people," he was saying.

"*These people* are incorrigible. I've come across them many times in my ministry down south and out west, and they're as stubborn and unrepentant as they were at the time they persecuted and betrayed the Lord. Even two thousand years of suffering haven't changed them. Even the Germans couldn't do anything with them. Now I'm not saying that it was right for the Germans to kill them, but I can understand how they got on the Germans' nerves with their stiff-necked, stubborn ways!"

I'm not saying that it was right for the Germans to kill them, BUT!!

It was as though a thousand pound stone had fallen on me. I sat there open-mouthed in disbelief and shock! Here in the *Beth Sar Shalom*, the very house of God, this red neck goy was spewing his anti-Semitic trash and not one person was interrupting or refuting him! Not one "brother" or "sister"!

Some months earlier, while walking in lower Manhattan, near Wall Street, I had come across a street preacher witnessing for "the Lord." He was talking about how Christians ought to unify in order to worship "the Lord" in purity and righteousness, not like the "dirty beards with the long black coats in the synagogues who think they are pleasing God by blowing their horns." I was angered by his words but told myself that this was just an ignorant goy, not a real Christian.

One of the most insidious and deceitful things missionaries do to the Jewish people is to deny Christian guilt for crimes Christians have committed against the Jews. Yet history books are full of these persecutions. Their apology for people like John Chrysostom in the Fifth Century or Father Coughlin in our own is that they were not true Christians. "True Christians would never harm anyone, least of all God's chosen Jewish people. Those who did harm Jews in the name of Jesus were imposters whom the devil had sent among the believers to give God's true church a bad name."

Yet an old Jewish proverb says: "He who acts in the name of a master is his disciple, and the master must bear the burden of the disciple's acts."

The Christian cross has been borne throughout the wide world accompanied by the Christian sword. Countless drops of blood have been shed in the name of Jesus. The Crusaders forced 500 Jewish men, women and children into a Jerusalem synagogue and then burned it to the ground while singing hymns of praise to the gentle Jesus, drowning out the screams of those perishing in the flames. Weren't those who did the burning and killing Christians?

Bill Travers told me that these Crusaders were Roman Catholics, i.e., gentile pagans (according to Bill) who desecrated the name of Jesus. Real Christians, like Martin Luther, he said, had recognized these pagans for what they were, and had therefore separated themselves from the Catholic Church. Martin Luther was a great man, Bill assured me, who had recognized the injustices done to God's chosen Jewish people.

In 1523, Martin Luther, the father of modern evangelical Protestantism, wrote a tract entitled, That *Jesus Christ was Born a Jew*, in which he said:

> Perhaps I will attract some of the Jews to the Christian faith. For our fools, the popes, bishops, and monks, the coarse blockheads, have until this time, so treated the Jews that to be a good Christian one would have to become a Jew. And if I had been a Jew and had seen such idiots ruling and teaching the Christian religion, I would rather have been a sow than

a Christian. I hope that, if the Jews are treated friendly and are instructed kindly through the Bible, many of them will become real Christians and come back to the ancestral faith of the prophets.

Yet twenty years of Christian "love" had failed to convert Jews. And in 1543, Martin Luther wrote in his tract, Concerning the Jews and their Lies:

> What then shall we Christians do with this damned, rejected race of Jews? Since they live among us and we know about their lying and blaspheming and cursing, we cannot tolerate them. Let me give you my honest advice. First, their synagogues or schools should be set on fire, and what does not burn should be covered or spread over with dirt so that no one may ever again be able to see a cinder or stone of it. Secondly, their homes should likewise be broken down and destroyed. Thirdly, they should be deprived of their prayer books and Talmuds. Fourthly, their rabbis must be forbidden, under threat of death, to teach any more ... that they may be prevented from uttering the name of God in our presence... We Christians can hardly believe that a Jew's foul mouth is worthy to speak the name of God in our presence; and if any of us should hear a Jew speak that name, he should at once inform the authorities or else throw pig shit at him.

In his Table Talks, Luther said things even more foul, repeatedly called Jews devils, and constantly compared Judaism to feces. At the Nuremberg trials, Julius Streicher was able to say about Luther: "We were only following his advice regarding the Jews." This same Martin Luther had been called a "great man" by my friend Bill Travers.

And what of those Christian leaders who were responsible for the religious guidance of the German people between 1933 and 1945? What did they have to say concerning their Hebrew-Christian brothers? On December 17, 1941, the Protestant Church Presidents and Bishops of Saxony, Mecklenburg, Schleswig Holstein, Thuringen, and Lubeck issued the following declaration:

> The National Socialist leaders of Germany have provided indisputable documentary evidence that the Jews are responsible for this war in its worldwide magnitude. They have therefore, made the necessary decisions and taken the necessary steps, both internal and external, to ensure that the life of the German nation is protected against Judaism. As members of that same German nation, the undersigned leaders of the German Evangelical Church stand in the forefront of this historical struggle to defend our country, because of which it has been necessary for the national police to issue a statement to the effect that the Jews are the enemies of the German nation and of the world, just as it was also necessary for Dr. Martin Luther to demand, on the basis of his own bitter experiences, that the severest measures should be taken against the Jews and that they should be expelled from all German countries...
>
> Christian baptism does not change in any way the Jew's racial character, his membership in the Jewish people and his biological nature. It is the duty of a German Evangelical Church

to foster and to promote the religious life of the German people. Christians who are Jews by race have no place in that Church and no right to a place. The undersigned leaders of the German Evangelical Church have therefore decided not to accept Jewish Christians as members of the Church community.

So much for the Christian clergyman under Hitler. But here and now, a bigot was spouting his mindless insults right in our very own *Beth Sar Shalom* and not one Hebrew-Christian had the integrity or presence of mind to oust him or at least to disagree with him.

I went home and thought long and hard about the Hebrew-Christians' attitude toward their fellow Jews. I, as a believer, so desperately needed affirmation as a Jew. Of course, Judaism itself would not grant me this. Most Hebrew-Christians told themselves that our Jewish people did not recognize us because of evil teaching by the rabbis. To support this view we could look at *Matthew 23* which paints a picture of rabbis as lacking the slightest shred of decency or human compassion.

The refusal of Jews to accept Jesus caused us Hebrew-Christians impatience, frustration, and anger. Other members of the *Beth Sar Shalom* told me that most unsaved Jews are atheists - especially the culture-bearers, the intellectuals, the liberals who have taken over the professions, banks, real estate, store chains, newspapers, entertainment media, and labor unions. Because they are in positions of power their unbelief makes them particularly dangerous. Those who are not atheists blindly follow antagonistic rabbis who denigrate Jesus and ridicule simple Christians. Whether atheists or not, Jews will suffer until they confess that the Messiah has already come. I was told that another major holocaust would occur in which the unbelieving Jews, (two-thirds of the Jewish people!) would die. Moreover, as *Romans, Chapter II* indicates, it is the unbelief of the Jews that postpones the coming of the Messianic kingdom.

I also heard that Jewish exclusiveness and separateness is irritating to gentiles, and cause continued hatred of Jews. I began to see that the Fundamentalist system we had accepted could foster anti-Semitism; it was sufficient to read texts like Matthew 27:25, John 8:42-47, 18:36, 19:7, 12-18, 1 Thessalonians 2:14-16, Titus 1:10.11 to realize that. But the most shocking thing to me was that many anti-Semitic statements like, "Jews think they are going to save themselves by stupid, petty rituals, like washing their hands before they eat bread," came from Hebrew-Christians.

It was ironic. Most Hebrew-Christians suffered more deeply from anti-Semitism than other Jews. They believed in the Gospels. Therefore they assumed the burden of that belief. "The Jews are the Chosen People;" they are also "the people who rejected and killed Christ." The "brothers" and "sisters" were constantly aware of this dual and paradoxical role to which Jews are assigned by the New Testament, - angels and devils. Because they considered themselves to be Jews, there was always present an element of distress, - the image of "Judas", the betrayer of Jesus, within themselves. They believed that the guilt for the Crucifixion lay upon the heads of "the Jews" (Matthew 17:25) and, even though they themselves had "made up" for this "ancestral crime" by accepting Jesus, still they often brooded about being thought of as "Christ-killers" by gentile believers. Therefore, they seemed to have a groveling, ingratiating attitude in the presence of *goyim*. I thought about my fellow Hebrew-Christians' inaction in the face of anti-Semitism in their midst and about my own inaction. It was unforgivable.

XIX

I
ESCAPE

By the summer of 1955, one of my sisters had married, and my brother had also left to live in his own apartment. Remaining at home were my oldest sister, my parents and me. My father had moved further from reality until he was no longer able to tolerate us nor we him. My mother took him to Family Court, and because he refused to "listen to reason," the court ordered him to leave our home. My father went to live with his sister and we began to think of looking for a new apartment for ourselves. By summer's end, my mother, sister, and I were ready to leave the neighborhood which had turned into a slum. We moved to an apartment in the West Bronx. With my father out of the picture, and the old apartment, with all of its unpleasant associations, left behind, I felt less tension. This was to be a new beginning for me.

I began to critically and objectively review my association with Hebrew-Christianity over the past year and a half. Initially I had accepted Jesus as the Jewish Messiah on the premise that by accepting him I would become a "completed Jew." The reality was that my accepting him had separated me from the larger Jewish community. I now realized why my family had not disowned me; it was not that they suffered from a lack of will, but that they loved me too much to throw me out. Even my father, as removed from reality as he was, had loved me in his own way; as angry as he had been at my acceptance of Christianity, he could not bring himself to ask me to leave.

But as a Hebrew-Christian I was truly neither fish nor fowl. I was, as are all Hebrew-Christians, a stranger in two worlds, constantly having to prove myself in both.

The "brothers" and "sisters" at *Beth Sar Shalom* were of no help to me. Most of them had come to Jesus, not as a positive religious experience, but as an escape from an alienating and sterile life. So given over to the "completed Jew" fantasy were they, that the memories of their pre-Christian lives had become caricatures. For example, I do not recall meeting one Jewish believer who did not declare that he or she had come from an "Orthodox" home. It turned out, however, that "Orthodox" simply meant a non-Christian, Yiddish-speaking, "bagels and lox" environment. Their stories of how they had been saved did not differ in kind, only in detail. It was a virtual litany of despair, describing how hopeless it all had been for them until Jesus came into their lives and took away the pain, the frustration, the boredom.

Verses prophesying Jesus as the Messiah? They no longer had any serious meaning for me. I had been saturated with verses, and I now knew that verses meant nothing by themselves. The meaning depended on interpretation, and even different sects of Christians disagreed about how verses should be interpreted. Jews had an entirely different understanding of the Bible from that of non-Jews. After all, Jews had studied the

Bible in the original Hebrew with all its special connotations, viewed it from different cultural milieus, and had the benefit of extensive rabbinical interpretations that reflected many centuries of scholarly study.

Christian theology? Impossibly uncomfortable for me. God born from a human mother? Revolting! A three-in one God? Comical! Hell's fire for my *zeyde* and *bobe*, and the six million? Criminal! A man might have devoted his entire life to improving the human condition, but because he was not a Christian, he was damned. A Hitler might accept Jesus a minute before his death and be saved. Peers? I would have to go to church to find peers. And they would not be Jewish. I would disappear as a Jew. I would become a goy. I would no longer be accepting Yeshua HaMeshiach, Jesus the Messiah. My God would be the gentile God, Jesus Christ, plain and simple.

And, however intensely I might profess love for that Jesus, I would still be the Christ-killer, the God-killer that John Villar had called me in the wash room at P.S. 61 when I was six years old and first heard of Jesus of Nazareth.

One day, during a subway ride to my home in the Bronx, a deep sigh escaped from my lips. My body went limp. Suddenly, I became aware that I could no longer believe in the Christian Messiah and remain Jewish. Joe Rocca had been right; as I had rejected Moses, so I now rejected Jesus. I knew that I must begin the long journey to rediscover Moses.

I arrived home and told my mother that I no longer believed in Jesus and that I would not be returning to the *Beth Sar Shalom*. Her reaction was as it had been on that Christmas day a year and a half earlier - not excited, but unemotional and quiet. She said gently, "From the day you first mentioned his name to me, I have been praying for you. Recently I had a dream. In it, your grandfather appeared. He said to me, 'Don't worry my daughter, the *Ribono-shel-olam*, the Master of the Universe, has heard your prayers.' And I know now that He has."

XX

A STRANGER
IN THE
HOUSE OF ISRAEL

The *Robono-shel-olam* had heard my mother's prayers. However, my "return" to Judaism was not to be as easy as I had anticipated.

Around the corner from where we lived was a Jewish book store. One day as I was passing by, I glanced at a book displayed in the window. It was Code of Jewish Law, an abridged codification of the standard Jewish legal work *Shulchan Aruch*. Excitedly, I bought a copy but when I took it home and looked inside, I was appalled! The minutiae of Orthodox obligations confronted me and I immediately felt intimidated. How could I, after experiencing the simplicity of Christianity; suddenly take on what is traditionally called the "yoke of the *Torah*?" I had no one to guide me. If this was what Judaism demanded, I could never live up to it. Christianity had taught me that "whosoever is under the Law is debtor to the whole of it;" that is, he is responsible for obeying the 613 commandments given to the Jewish people through Moses.

Several days later I returned to the bookstore and purchased a *siddur*, the book of daily prayers. The liturgy made no sense to me even with the accompanying English translation. The prayers seemed to go on and on endlessly. No simple hymns here. How could anyone be expected to squeeze so many words into the course of a day? And yet, praying to God ought to be the easiest thing of all, I thought. If I can't even do that, how can I perform all the other demanding, complicated *Torah* rituals? I did not know where to turn. I needed to be with other Jews who knew what it was all about. Surely, they would help me experience genuine Judaism with at least as much zeal as the *Beth Sar Shalom* people had helped me experience what I now felt to be ersatz Judaism. How naive I was!

Several blocks from where we lived was a Reform temple. I decided to go there the next Saturday morning. Unfortunately, I found the services at the temple to be very disappointing. There was little of the spontaneous religious feeling I had felt at the *Beth Sar Shalom*. Both the hymns and the English prayers were drab. The rabbi's sermon was uninspiring. It was all very decorous and, to me, completely sterile. Were it not for an occasional Hebrew sentence in transliteration, I could easily have been sitting in a Protestant church.

I attended services at the temple two Saturdays in a row. I was obviously a stranger, a new face. Yet no one in the place, not even the rabbi, approached me to find out who I was or what had brought me there.

How sweet and how good it is for brothers to sit together.
Psalms 133:1

What irony that the "brothers" and "sisters" at the *Beth Sar Shalom* understood that verse so much better than the people here in this "temple" of God. Their lack of interest, especially in the light of what I had experienced over the past year and a half, was a blow to me. But my desire to be united religiously with the House of Israel made it easy to rationalize this away. These were Reform Jews, I could say. Of course they lacked the warmth and exuberance of more traditional Jews. If I went to a traditional synagogue rather than to a Reform temple, the Jews there would know how to act toward me.

Several weeks later, I was passing by an Orthodox synagogue on the Grand Concourse. On impulse I went in. I wanted to be with my fellow Jews that day. I realized that my head was not covered, so I approached a man who was obviously one of the synagogue officials to ask for a *yarmulke*, skullcap. He hardly looked at me as he answered abruptly, "We have no hats here. You are not dressed properly and your head is not covered. You don't look right. Please leave."

I was shocked! No one stood up for me. No one said anything. No one even offered to look for a spare *yarmulke*. It was as though my own brother had stuck a knife in me.

I yelled out, "You son of a bitch! On the day you die, maybe you won't look right to God!" I turned my back to the startled stares around me and stormed out.

That day was *Yom Kippur* of 1955. I was not to step back into a synagogue for over ten years.

Part III

The fool hath said in his heart, There is no God.

Psalms 14:1

The secret things belong unto the Lord our God; but those things which are revealed belong to us.

Deuteronomy 29:29

As for the son who does not know how to ask, you must guide him.

Passover Haggadah

XXI
SEARCHING FOR GOD

In the spring of 1956, I purchased a copy of Man and His *Gods: The Story of Man's Religious Philosophies and Their Influences* by Homer W. Smith, a biologist at New York University. This book had a significant effect on my thinking regarding religion. It started me on a search to confirm what Smith had written. My intent here is not to summarize his book; rather, I want to highlight what impressed me.

While I now realize that Smith had a strong bias against all religion and that much of what he wrote was anti-religious polemic, I found his arguments convincing when I first read them.

Smith first chronicled the development of religious ideas in Egypt and Mesopotamia, and described what he calls "Hebrew traditions and morality." He employed what is commonly known as "Biblical Criticism".

After reviewing Jewish history up to the time of King Josiah, he described the religious revival effected in Judah by that king. Josiah rooted out and destroyed the last vestiges of idolatry among the inhabitants of the land of Israel, and it was during his reign that the book of Deuteronomy was rediscovered in the Temple at Jerusalem by priests who were helping in the reconstruction of the Sanctuary. Josiah stringently enforced the laws dealing with idolaters; their punishment was death and total destruction of their property. The Jews renewed their ancient covenant with God and pledged to live faithfully in accordance with His laws. Professor Smith stated, "When the king and his people entered the Temple and 'made a covenant ... to perform the words of this covenant that were written in this book,' the gates of the most enduring walls ever to imprison men - the Hebraic Law - shut silently behind them." Professor Smith, a non-Christian and certainly not an anti-Semite, was making a negative judgment of the *Torah*. Of course, I realized that he was doing this in order to strike at the Christian interpretation of the *Torah* Nevertheless, the fact that a scholar could view the *Torah* as a prison made an impression on me. It was the late 1950s, after all, and wasn't the world becoming increasingly secular? And weren't Jews in the forefront of that secularization process? Perhaps "old-time religion" was really passé. I read on.

Smith spoke about the gods of classical antiquity. The Greco-Roman world had been filled with savior gods who after death (which was sometimes by being impaled on wood), had been resurrected and thus ensured eternal life to their devotees. So I saw that Jesus had not been the only so-called "dying and rising god" in history. Smith pointed out that, as to be expected, the church fathers, who had always blamed their misfortunes on Satan, now accused the devil of having anticipated Christianity and imitating it in advance in the form of pagan cults. As for the Gospels, Smith showed that they were written long after Jesus' death, and filled with discrepancies and interpolations of various editors. Smith pointed out that it was not clear from unbiased, that is, secular history, that Jesus had even existed, or if he had, that he had died in the manner portrayed by the Gospels. Smith's arguments supported my rejection of Jesus and Christian beliefs. Smith described the church's role in history; how it did nothing to prevent the disintegration of law and morality in the Roman Empire, how it even abetted the disintegration, and how it practiced unbridled cruelty on outsiders as well as on its own followers. I was disgusted. Especially offensive to me was that, in a facile manner, the Gospels attributed everything that it could not bring into conformity with its own beliefs and practices as being of Satan. This "devil" whom it elevated to the status of a god of evil was opposed forever to the Christian God Christ.

I learned that eight to ten million gentile Europeans, prompted by Satan not to accept Jesus as Saviour, were put to death by the Christian sword; that differences of opinion with official church dogma, called "heresies", were ruthlessly suppressed in the name of the "prince of peace." During the sixteenth century and continuing for almost three hundred years afterwards, for example, the church instituted systematic persecutions of those whom it called witches. This persecution was carried on to such a degree of horror that it can only be compared in scope with the Christian persecution of the Jewish people. It is probably this section of Smith's book, dealing with the church's treatment of a group of defenseless women, more than any other part, which caused me to experience revulsion toward religion.

> I turned and saw the oppressions that are done under the sun;
> And behold the tears of such as were oppressed,
> and they had no comforter;
> And on the side of their oppressors there was power,
> But they had no comforter.
> *Ecclesiastes 4:1*

These lines are attributed to King Solomon, who lived about one thousand years before the Christian era. Those who now claimed to receive their inspiration from the same Source as did Solomon, were indeed themselves the oppressors. The appearance of Protestantism did not alleviate the situation. In fact, it made things worse. Whereas Catholics had relied on Church law in their fight against Satan and his agents, Protestants depended directly on their own interpretation of Scripture. They concluded that witches were not to be left alive lest they seduce people away from the worship of God. The history of New England alone reveals how zealous these "Reformers" were when it came to "beating the devil." It was cruelty inflicted on innocent and helpless victims. How could such behavior have been sanctioned by Heaven? Where were love and compassion in all of this? Those who did not think right or look right were outside the realm of religious compassion, at least to these Christians.

It seemed that those who looked and thought right had a private line to God. Such persons thought they had all the answers. We Jews did not persecute and torture. We did not spread our religion by the sword and the rack. But then, we had been politically powerless to spread our religion by any means.

Homer Smith wrote that other peoples, who existed, before the Jews became a nation, also thought they were aware of Divine truths. The Babylonians, for example, had the story of *Uta-Napishtim*, a man who built an ark and saved himself and his family when the gods sent a flood to cover the earth. They knew of Marduk, who cut the dragon Tiamat in half when he created the world just as Jehovah had sundered Tehom, the deep, when He ushered in creation. But geologists claimed that the world was not created in six days. Rather, it had evolved. The ancient Semites knew nothing of evolution. They shared a common collection of myths to explain how life came about.

We were the heirs of these myths, perhaps in a form less crude, but myths nonetheless. And belief in these myths, not love or compassion, welded men together. And to impress these myths upon our minds, they had become ritualized. Even prayer, talking to God, had become ritualized. There was no spontaneity. Right belief, right performance of ritual, right appearance had become the essence of religion. These had replaced God. God was no longer part of religion - not that God who, I had been told, cared for the widow, the orphan, the stranger, the oppressed; the God who was Love. He did not exist. He no longer existed for me. As Joe Rocca had been right in predicting that I would eventually give up Jesus, so now it appeared Bill Travers had also been correct in saying that I would give up everything, Jesus, Judaism, faith.

In the fall of 1956, Bill called me to see how I was doing. I told him how I felt in no uncertain terms. I had had it. I slammed down the receiver. I never heard from him again. This indicated to me that Bill was interested in knowing what progress I was making in the Christian religion. He was not interested in me as a person or as a friend.

XXII
I CONTINUE MY SEARCH

I spent the late 1950s and early 1960s in "information gathering." I read the writings of various humanists and was particularly impressed with those of Thomas Paine. His Age of Reason refuted in detail the myth that so-called "Old Testament" verses contain prophesies about Jesus being the Messiah. (Subsequently, I discovered further confirmation of this in the writings of both Jews and gentiles.) Yet, by his own testimony, Paine did not condemn any who believed in their respective churches. As a humanist and universalist, he was far kinder to the "religious" than they were to him. Thomas Paine represented the type of reasonable and honorable man I could admire.

I also became interested in what psychoanalysis had to say about religious phenomena. In particular, I pored over the works of Sigmund Freud and Theodore Reik dealing with Jewish and Christian religious themes. Freud, of course, saw religion as an impediment to civilization, since it stifled people and encouraged them to suppress natural urges. This led to neurosis, according to Freud, and he foresaw a time when mankind would no longer need the "crutch" of faith. He argued further that the concept of God originated in the oedipal strivings of tribal males who rebelled against the Ur- father in order to deprive him of exclusive possession of the tribal females. All was the result of sex.

Reik dealt more specifically with Jewish ritual and lore. For him the Jewish religion emerged from primitive adolescent initiation rites. Such theories now appear simple and contrived to me, but then they made a considerable impression and seemed plausible. After all, if I would not question the wisdom of men like Homer Smith or Thomas Paine, how much less likely was I to question, or even doubt, such thinkers as Freud or Reik?

In 1958, I joined The Freethinkers' Society of America, a militantly atheistic organization dedicated to the proposition that morality and ethical behavior can be taught, transmitted, and sustained by a culture outside the religious context, and unconnected to the idea of a Divinely given law.

I began to buy more books on religion, psychology, and philosophy. Even after I was drafted into the Army in the spring of 1960, I spent much of my small monthly pay on books. Once I read a book, I would ship it home. My mother's letters complained about the lack of storage space in her apartment and how foolishly I squandered my pay. But I kept reading.

XXIII
PREJUDICE
IN THE ARMY

While with the U.S. Army 17th Signal Battalion in Karlsruhe, Germany, I first came in contact with a broad cross section of American youth, and the amount of raw prejudice I observed, both anti-Black and anti-Semitic, was disturbing. The Army's unofficial attitude was resigned acceptance. They seemed to reason that prejudice was part of human nature, and that it will surface when men of diverse backgrounds are made to live together for lengthy periods. Ugly incidents resulted, and sometimes even those instigated by noncommissioned officers were simply ignored. As far as I could tell, the anti-Semitic occurrences did not result from religious convictions. Rather, they were expressions of mindless hatred for its own sake - hatred of the Jewish people, not for anything we supposedly had done two thousand years ago, but simply because we existed.

I was in a country where scarcely fifteen years earlier, millions of innocent people had been killed simply because "human nature" was allowed to surface. And I was now part of an army, some of whose members openly hailed the Nazi, George Lincoln Rockwell, as a hero. The U.S. Army occupied the land that had produced the Third Reich and the "Final Solution". Yet I was certain that many of my fellow soldiers, if they had lived during the 1930's and 1940's, had been given swastika armbands, and told to go along with such annihilations, would have readily done so.

I do not mean to indict either the United States Army or its soldiers in general. The overwhelming majority of those men with whom I spent two years of my life, were decent human beings. But the number of potential fascists among them loomed too large for comfort, especially since the ovens of Dachau, only a two hour train ride away, had hardly cooled.

But this firsthand experience with anti-Semitism also made a positive impact. It caused me to reexamine my Jewishness and to question why some non-Jews are so prejudiced.

Meanwhile, in Germany, people were still talking about the capture of Adolph Eichmann by the Israelis, which had occurred on May 23, 1960, a month after I had entered the army. This event, in my opinion, initiated a new era in Jewish history. I did not realize it then, but Eichmann's capture helped prepare Jews to advocate a more outspoken position vis-a-vis their enemies. Just consider the psychological and emotional uplift it gave to Soviet Jewry's dissident movement. This attitude was also evident during the Six Day War, the raid at Entebbe, the bombing of the nuclear reactor in Bagdad, and the invasion of Lebanon. It evoked a Jewish consciousness among many Israelis who had once considered themselves as Jews only peripherally and coincidentally. It also heightened the self-awareness of Jews living throughout the Diaspora. And it suppressed, at least for the time being, those bullies who become more strident when they think their enemy is weak.

It signaled a new response to anti-Semitism. Jews began to assert their concern for each other in ways so dramatic that they were unparalleled. Such events contributed to my ultimate decision to turn to the fold of committed Jewry.

In April, 1961, I received word through the Red Cross that my father had passed away. By the time I was contacted, my father had already been buried, and my family therefore felt that it wasn't necessary for me to fly home from Germany. I concurred. So alienated had my father become from us, that I did not even think of observing the traditional periods of mourning.

XXIV
MY JEWISH CONCERNS

In 1964, I was living in Manhattan's Greenwich Village. I had continued to amass books and the shelves of my one-room apartment were lined with books on Jewish history, philosophy, literature, and other aspects of Jewish life. My friends told me that I was afflicted with bibliomania, and that soon I would have nowhere to sleep because I'd have to use my bed as a bookshelf. The problem was that I lived in a world of Jewish books, and not in a world peopled with observant Jews.

One day as I was walking along Sixth Avenue near Eighth Street, a young man wearing a yarmulke handed me a flyer. It announced a forthcoming rally outside the Russian Embassy on behalf of the "Jews of Silence" who were being held captive by the Soviets. The rally was to protest the spiritual genocide being conducted against Jews by the Russian government. As the son of immigrants from the Ukraine, I was well aware of how terribly Jews had been treated in Russian lands before the 1917 revolution. But since that time, the Soviets had declared anti-Semitism to be a crime against the state. Yet even after having fought a war against Nazi Germany, the Russians were apparently still carrying on the old Czarist-Cossack tradition of hatred towards Jews, but in a more sophisticated way.

I attended the rally and listened to speeches by various politicians. I also heard impassioned pleas by such Jewish personalities as Shlomo Riskin, rabbi of Lincoln Square Synagogue in Manhattan, and Jacob Birnbaum and Glen Richter, founders of the Center for Russian Jewry and the Student Struggle for Soviet Jewry. I was not familiar with any of these speakers, but their eloquence and fiery concern for fellow Jews impressed me.

Here was a demonstration, in every sense of the word, of Jewish brotherly love. Here were American Jews of all ages coming together to aid their brethren thousands of miles away. The Jews of the Soviet Union did not have to "look right" to have the support of these brothers and sisters assembled on a street of Manhattan's East Side. They just had to be Jews in trouble. We were determined not to let them down.

XXV
GROPING TOWARD JUDAISM

One day during the summer of 1966 I noticed an ad in the *New York Daily News*. It read:

LAWS OF MOSES
CONFIRMED BY MODERN SCIENCE!
For further details, write for our booklet showing how the Bible gives us a blueprint for better living.

I sent for the booklet. It turned out to be the first lesson of a correspondence course on the Bible. The booklet pointed out the hackneyed facts about certain foods containing trichinosis, etc., and how the Mosaic Law told people to avoid them, in order to prolong their lives. Subsequent booklets went on to describe true worship; that is, worship of the Deity alone and not of intermediaries or angels. By the fifth booklet it was obvious where the course program was leading; it was a ploy to "prove" to the uninformed that Jesus is Israel's Messiah.

So they were still around. I decided I had nothing to lose. They were even paying the postage. Each time I returned the completed test questionnaire at the end of a booklet, I accompanied it with questions and notes refuting the Christological "prophecies" and pointed out the New Testament inconsistencies.

But the correspondents were not deterred. They had a counterargument for each of my arguments. Thought and prayer would show me the way, they assured me.

After about six months, correspondence stopped. They must have run out of material - or patience. Meanwhile, I decided that as a Jew it was my duty to become thoroughly familiar with the Bible. After all, it was our book, even though it was constantly being used against us by certain Christians. The pity was that every Jew I knew was a biblical ignoramus. I had previously devoted my studies to the various aspects of Jewish life. Now I decided to concentrate on Jewish religion - beginning with the Bible. But my quest was still not to be supported by my fellow Jews.

The eve of *Yom Kippur*, 1966.

I had a date late that afternoon. We were walking along Central Park West, enjoying the balmy weather of a lingering Indian Summer. Nearing the corner of 71st Street, we noticed some Orthodox Jews who were dressed up and on their way to a nearby synagogue. On impulse, I asked my date, a Jewish woman, whether she would like to hear Kol Nidrei, the moving prayer that opens the *Yom Kippur* service. She said she would and so we went over to this synagogue. But as we were entering, a man dressed in a tuxedo stopped us and asked whether we had High Holiday tickets. I explained that we did not but that we only wanted to stay long enough to hear Kol Nidrei. The man smiled politely and said he was sorry but that would be impossible. This time there was no problem about not having a head covering or the proper dress. No one said that we didn't look right. These Jews were too sophisticated for that. This time it was a matter of "fire safety regulations." Only those who had paid for and reserved seats could be safely accommodated in the building. A polite "sorry." That's all!

Nothing further was said. No invitation was extended to return on the following Sabbath. Here was the same lack of concern I sensed in other *shuls*. There was no reaching out, no caring, and no giving a damn. We were obviously not living in a time that would hasten the coming of the Messiah. Before that would happen, the *arelut*, the uncircumcised covering, would have to melt away from the hearts of Jews who called themselves 'religious'. A sense of caring would have to develop.

My disappointment made me feel like screaming at the man in the tuxedo but I restrained myself. As we walked away from the synagogue, my date seemed to sense my frustration. "They really could have let us stay there for just a few minutes, I suppose," she murmured.

Such negative experiences with "religious" Jews could have turned me away forever. But something continued to attract me to Judaism. As we walked toward my apartment that evening, I could not know that my life was about to change very dramatically.

XXVI
I MEET AN OBSERVANT JEW

I usually carry a book with me everywhere so that I can read on the subway, in checkout lines, or at any other opportunity. Toward the end of 1966, I began to buy the Soncino books of the Bible; they are bilingual editions, each containing a verse-by-verse commentary, mainly classical, such as Rashi (Rabbi Solomon Ben Isaac) and Rambam (Maimonides). I was then working as a salesman in a midtown department store, and I would read on my breaks in the store's cafeteria. One day I was engrossed in the book of Deuteronomy, when a salesman about my age from another department walked into the cafeteria and sat down at my table. He introduced himself as Michael Kahan. I was annoyed because he was disturbing my reading, but there was something likeable about him.

Mike said that he was amazed to see someone spending his break reading, of all things, Deuteronomy. He was especially surprised to see someone reading it that was Jewish but obviously not religious. When I asked him why he thought I wasn't religious, he answered that no religious Jew would be reading the Hebrew Bible with his head uncovered. I was embarrassed, but noticing my unease, he immediately apologized. He didn't want to make me feel uncomfortable, he said, but was just stating the obvious, perhaps overstating it, he added. In any case, he was impressed that a fellow Jew was reading something worthwhile instead of the "nonsense that nowadays passes for books." As for himself, he said that he had recently become an observant Jew and was trying to get his family to become observant also.

I was impressed and curious. Why had he undertaken such an ambitious enterprise? And how was his family reacting to his "finding religion?"

Mike laughed and said his family was very tolerant, and since his mother kept a kosher home, it wasn't that difficult. Fortunately, the rabbi at the Sephardic synagogue in his neighborhood - a man interested in bringing young people back to Judaism - was helping him.

Then he became particularly intense. He leaned forward and looking directly at me, said, "Religious or not, never forget you're a Jew, a member of a great people. We're all one - Ashkenazi, Sephardi, Hasid, or *Mitnagid.* Hitler showed us that, but we should have known before he showed us. You know," he raised his voice slightly, "the *goyim* are jealous because we're Chosen."

I looked around quickly to see who had heard. The cafeteria was fairly crowded, but no one seemed concerned with us.

"Don't worry about them," he said in the same pitch, as his tone became challenging. "Any one of these *goyim* who doesn't like it can try to do something about it."

I was shocked! True, he was physically a big man, but even so, to speak aloud like that! I had never heard this done by any Jew before. He became defiant. "You know, most *goyim* are anti-Semitic mamzerim!" My face was red, but he paid no attention. "Just remember," he exclaimed. "All we have is each other, and God. Be proud I wanted to feel proud, but all I could manage was to feel embarrassed.

But the truth of the matter was that I began to look up to Mike as a model of a type of Jew who was proud of his Jewishness; who felt strong convictions, and who was not afraid of voicing them. In a somewhat secular sense, he became my "rabbi" for a time. We became close friends after I became accustomed to his candor He taught me to stand a little taller and somewhat prouder as a Jew. Unfortunately, he was not able to influence me to start becoming more observant because I had not yet attained either the discipline or the inclination to learn. Still his chauvinism was infectious.

XXVII
A HEBREW-CHRISTIAN DINNER

Early in April 1967, a man with an attaché case rang my bell. He introduced himself as Mr. someone-or other from the *Beth Sar Shalom*. He was sweating even though it hadn't turned warm yet. He told me that he had obtained my name from a Seventh Day Adventist group that had sent me a Bible study correspondence course. I smiled. So they had not forgotten about me when they stopped writing. They had decided to turn my case over to "other Jews." The gentleman told me there was to be an annual dinner of the American Board of Missions to the Jews at a well-known midtown Manhattan hotel on Saturday night, June 3rd. H extended an invitation to me to attend and meet other Jews who had found their Messiah.

It had been twelve years since I left the *Beth Sar Shalom*, and very few times since then had I thought about that period. I was embarrassed about that part of my life. But my curiosity got the better of me. More than that, I felt that perhaps I could engage in "fact gathering" on the Hebrew-Christians, and turn the data over to some Jewish organization, perhaps the Anti-Defamation League. The idea was somewhat nebulous in my mind, but still I decided to accept the invitation.

The dinner was held in a large room. About 100 persons were in attendance, but there was no one I recognized from the *Beth Sar Shalom*. This was indicative of the instability of the Hebrew-Christian movement; few members stayed with it for very long. While constantly seeking to recruit new members, those already recruited either move on to a church or drop out somewhere along the way.

Aside from the two gentile group leaders seated alongside me, two women in their twenties and an older married couple were at my table. The four of them were Jewish, but to my surprise, they were not Hebrew Christians. The two women were sitting directly across from me, giving me hostile looks. When I asked them what was the matter, one of them sneeringly asked me if I were a Hebrew-Christian. She pronounced the word Hebrew-Christian with sarcasm thick enough to cut. So that was it. For some reason, these women had also come along "for the ride." When I assured them I wasn't a Hebrew-Christian, they relaxed and became friendly. It turned out they were Reconstructionist, and were in New York for the summer, taking courses at the Jewish Theological Seminary.

As the gentile group leaders talked with us, they repeated the already familiar Christian claim that the Talmud was a device rabbis used to keep the Jews ignorant of their true religion, i.e., Christianity. They said the rabbis wanted the Jews to busy themselves learning complicated, man-made interpretations of the Bible in order to obscure the pure simplicity of the Bible itself. If only Jews would put aside the Talmudic shield covering their eyes, they would clearly see the true Judaism that Jesus preached.

The two women pointedly ignored them, but I felt that the group leaders had a nerve, being gentiles, to impugn our religious tradition and the rabbis, and I told them so. They replied that they had meant no offense, but were simply trying to say that observing ritualistic minutiae would not justify a person before God. Since my knowledge of Judaism up to now was limited, I found it very difficult to argue with them. I muttered something to the effect that mere belief did not justify a person before God. The group leaders then noticed that the women weren't touching anything on their plates. When they asked them about this, their response was that the food was not kosher. The two gentiles became embarrassed and said they were sorry that they hadn't thought about that earlier. The truth of the matter, however, was obvious to us; they had never expected anyone with genuine Jewish commitment to show up at the dinner.

When the meal was finished, everyone stood up for the concluding prayer. The prayer consisted of two petitions: first, that God allow the Jews to have "the blindness which is the Talmud" removed from their eyes, and second, that He stand by Israel in her hour of need now that Arab neighbors seemed about to attack her from all sides. The order of the priorities was clear!

The prayer over, the two gentiles wished God's blessings on us and left the table. We Jews sat there, reminded of the bitter reality of the past two weeks. The Egyptians and the Syrians were poised to strike against Israel in the Sinai and along the Golan Heights. United Nations forces had been withdrawn from the area without a word, indicating already the UN's moral collapse. The Arabs had given further provocation to the Jewish State with their blockade of the Tiran Straits, and king Hussein was hysterically arousing the Jordanians to kill Jews wherever they found them.

We began to discuss the situation. The women were frankly worried and asked the married couple, who had remained silent throughout the dinner, and me, to come to a solidarity rally for Israel that was to be held the next day, Sunday, in Manhattan's Riverside Park. The couple said they would not be able to attend because they were leaving New York for an out of town medical conference scheduled to begin on Monday; the husband, a physician and a well-known expert in the field of homosexuality and transsexualism, was delivering a paper at the conference.

The doctor and his wife did not seem overly concerned with the gravity of what was happening in the Middle East. They felt that the situation would be defused before any hostilities occurred. The Arabs were making a lot of noise, they said, but Nasser would remember what happened in 1956 when the Egyptians had been completely routed in the Sinai. All Israel had to do was to flex its muscles a little and the Egyptians would retreat, and without Egypt, Syria and Jordan would do nothing. But the women were not convinced. The Arabs intended another Holocaust, they said, and no one seemed to care.

I became uncomfortable. I asked, "Where are all our Christian "friends"? Why have the church leaders shut their mouths? Why isn't President Johnson doing anything? The doctor assured me there was nothing to worry about. "Don't you realize," he asked, "that Israel had the strongest, best trained army in the Middle East? Even if the Arabs do attack," he said, "they don't stand a chance of winning a war with Israel." But the rest of us were not so sure. All we could think of at the moment was the silence of the gentiles in the face of another Auschwitz.

The doctor and his wife asked if we would like to go for a drive. The five of us got into their car, and we drove along the Henry Hudson Parkway on that warm June night, hardly speaking. Finally, we talked and explained our reasons for coming to the Hebrew Christian dinner in the first place. The women and the doctor and his wife had, like me, answered that newspaper ad concerning the Mosaic dietary laws and had taken the correspondence course. They had been contacted by the *Beth Sar Shalom*, invited to the dinner, and out of curiosity had accepted the invitation. The women told me they wanted to "see the missionaries up close." As for the doctor and his wife, they said they would try anything new.

The rally in Riverside Park proved to be a great success, with over 50,000 Jews in attendance. It was the Soviet Jewry rally I had attended some three years earlier all over again, but now on a more grandiose scale. Jews really did care about one another. "Kawl yisrael Khaverim!" ("All Jews are brothers!") "Kawl yisrael aravim ze el ze!" ("All Jews are responsible for one another!") And so is God, I hoped.

Later that evening, I went up to the Bronx to see my friend, Mike Kahan. We sat drinking coffee, and talked about Israel and the silence of the *goyim*. Mike asked me, "Do you believe in those biblical books you've been reading?"

"I'm trying to," I answered, "but it's hard. I've been without a God-feeling for a long time."

"Look," he said, "it's like this. The *goyim* don't want us around but I could care less about what they don't want this time. Jews didn't go into the fire for nothing. God promised through his prophets that at the last days Israel would be reestablished and would endure.

"Israel has come back to its land. No matter what they try to do or don't do, we have His word."

The next day, Monday, June 5th, I awoke and turned on the radio. I was stunned! The Israeli military had destroyed the Egyptian air force and was advancing into the Sinai, up the Golan, and across the Jordan Valley, The Arabs were fleeing in terror before the sword of Judah!

XXVIII
APOCALYPSE, JUNE 1967

Ye shall lie down, and none shall make you afraid.
And ye shall chase your enemies,
And they shall fall before you by the sword.
And five of you shall chase a hundred,
And a hundred of you shall put ten thousand to flight.
And your enemies shall fall before you by the sword.

Leviticus 26:6-8

By Saturday, June 10, 1967, it was over. Jewish soldiers were sitting on the Golan Heights. They had reached the Suez Canal and the Jordan River. But above all, Jews were praying at the Temple Wall. I felt that an apocalypse had occurred. I felt the reality of the Bible.

Most Jews felt the living reality of the Bible. It was Moses at the Red Sea, Joshua at Ajalon, Gideon at Gilead, Samson at Gaza, David at Jerusalem, Judah Maccabee at the gates of the Temple all over again.

Something inside me turned on. For the first time in over a decade I felt the reality of God; I felt Him moving in history again. He was speaking to the Jewish people again after long years of silence; He was speaking to the world again. All that the world needed to do was listen.

But there were those who chose not to hear. As the heart of Pharaoh had become hard, so had the hearts of the nations grown hard?

Why do the nations rage,
and the people imagine a vain thing?
The kings of the earth set themselves,
And the rulers take counsel together,
Against the Lord,
and against His anointed people, saying,
Let us break their fetters asunder,
And cast away their cords from us.
He that sitteth in the heavens shall laugh.
The Lord shall hold them in derision.

Psalms 2:1-4

But if the majority of the non-Jewish world refused to listen, we had to listen. It was clear now. We were not able to depend on them. We were neither to follow after them nor to take on their ways. We had a destiny. Again, after more than ten years, I felt that sense of Jewish destiny, of choosiness, of the specialness of the Jews that my mother had instilled in me as a child. If God had indeed chosen us, then we had to respond to that election. I knew now that the world hated us for being the Chosen People. One had only to read the newspapers in the months that followed the Six Day War to see that hatred manifested in the council of nations. The state of Israel had become isolated in the world; the people of Israel shared that isolation.

But those who did not hate us stood and marveled. And the words of the gentile prophet, Balaam, echoed across the ages.

How shall I curse whom God hath not cursed?
Or how shall I defy whom the Lord hath not defied?
For from the tops of the rocks I see him,
And from the hills I behold him.
Behold, it is a people which will dwell alone
And it shall not be counted among the nations.
                              Numbers 23:8-9

How goodly are thy tents,
O Jacob, and thy Tabernacles,
O Israel As the valleys are, they spread forth.
As gardens by the river's side
As the trees of align aloes which the Lord hath planted
As the cedars beside the waters.
                              Numbers 24:5-6

God brought him forth out of Egypt;
He hath the strength of a wild-ox.
He shall eat up the nations his enemies,
And shall break their bones,
And shall pierce them through with His arrows.
He couched down
He lay down as a lion, and as a great lion.
Who will stir him up?
Blessed is he that blesseth thee,
And cursed is he that curseth thee..
                              Numbers 24:8-9

There shall come a star out of Jacob,
And a scepter shall rise out of Israel,
And smite the corners of Moab,
And destroy all the foundations thereof
And Edom shall be his possession,
Seir also,
His enemies shall be his possession,
And Israel shall do valiantly.

Numbers 24:17-18

XXIX
OF CONVERTS AND MISSIONARIES

Abraham Carmel, who recently passed away, was an Angilican priest who became Jewish. Like Abraham of old, he smashed his idols and left his country, his kindred, and the house of his fathers, and joined himself to the Jewish people.

I first heard of Dr. Carmel through an acquaintance of mine who had heard him speak in a synagogue in Far Rockaway, New York. I had met Jews who had converted to Christianity, but I had never met anyone who had converted to Judaism.I was intrigued by the idea that someone who had been a priest and a member of the comfortable British middle class could so drastically alter his circumstances and his life-style. Mike Kahan and I decided to contact him and arrange to meet him.

Dr. Carmel agreed to meet with us at a dairy restaurant on West 49th Street in Manhattan. He even offered to treat us to dinner. The meeting took place on a Sunday evening in the spring of 1968. Dr. Carmel displayed a quiet dignity and extreme humility, and Mike and I liked him instantly. We had a battery of questions for him, and he had a great deal of patience with us.

We asked him why he had decided to become a Jew when he had had all the advantages of remaining a Christian in a Christian society, a member of the majority civilization. He answered that he had made the decision after years of careful contemplation and study. He had originally converted to Catholicism, he said, in order to get closer to the religious source, but apparently it had not been close enough. What he learned of Jewish tradition and Jewish history was too much at variance with what the Church taught. Soon such concepts as the Trinity and Transubstantiation (the belief that during communion the bread and wine are transformed into the body and blood of Jesus) became unacceptable to him. He could no longer officiate at the Mass. Dr. Carmel left the priesthood and later the Church, and undertook a religious quest to discover the true nature of God.

Like Moses, he had asked to be shown the Divine glory, and had later come to understand that unlike the Christian view of God, the face of the Jewish God cannot be seen in this life. It remains hidden in transcendence. It is permitted to man only to glimpse some aspect of the Creator in retrospect. God places His hand over our eyes, so to speak, as he acts in the present time but removes it once He has acted. It is for us then to discern His "back" in what has passed us by, such as Divine influence in the Six Day War.

A rearward glimpse of the Deity had been sufficient for Dr. Carmel. He threw in his lot with the Jewish people.

We asked him if there was any difference in the relationship between him and his family now that he was Jewish. He nodded and, in his quiet way, said, "Yes, there is a gulf. My family is respectful towards me, but whenever I go back to England to visit, I feel the strain."

Then I asked him how he felt about Jewish missionary movements comparable to those of the Christians. His answer has stuck with me ever since. He said, "Conversion to Judaism is not the same as conversion to Christianity. One does not become a Jew in order to gain eternal salvation, since we believe that 'the righteous of all the nations have a share in the world to come.' No. One becomes a Jew in order to attain to a priestly level of serving God, to have a share in His *Torah* Law. Secondly, Christianity seeks to convert nations. Conversion to Judaism is a personal and private affair between the individual and the Almighty. It is a one-to-one relationship. And finally, you should be aware of this: two thousand years ago when Paul set out to convert the gentiles, they were not ready to receive the *Torah*, today they are still not ready. If we would be missionaries, then let us first missionize our own young Jews, so many of whom have sold their birth right for what amounts to a pot of beans. Let us draw them near to *Torah* and its Giver."

Mike and I were awed by Dr. Carmel, by his humility, his sincerity, and his commitment. Here was someone who "knew the heart of the stranger," and who was telling us to reach out to estranged Jews, alienated youth, in our midst. But in order to reach out, we had to be involved. I, for one, was still only involved with the abstract idea of my Jewishness, not with a daily commitment to living in accordance with Jewish precepts.

XXX
THOSE WHO
STEAL THE MIND

I knew that something was lacking in my life. It was that "daily commitment to living in accordance with Jewish precepts" that I had felt at the time of my meeting with Abraham Carmel. I wanted to do something about giving my life more Jewish content but I did not know where or how to begin. This was the period just before the great *Baal T'shuvah*, Return of the Repentants movement within Judaism. Furthermore, memories of too many negative associations to establishment Jewish religious institutions caused me to hold back from making any active moves.

In addition, something I witnessed during the summer of 1968 caused me a great deal of pain. It was an example of what, unfortunately, still continues to exist as a stumbling block in the eyes of many Jews who would like to come closer to God. It was an example, too of what gives ammunition to anti-religious Jews.

That summer I was taking an evening psychology course at City College of New York while working during the day. Two young Jewish men in my class sat in the back of the room. Although I did not have an opportunity to speak to them during the course of the semester, but I assumed they were Orthodox since they wore yarmulkes.

Finals were approaching, and I was cramming for this course as well as for another. A day before the exam I discovered that these two young Jews had obtained a copy of the exam as well as the answers. I overheard them talking and laughing about it at the back of the room. I began to boil. I was struggling to pass the course, and these two had the nerve to laugh about how they were going to use unfair and immoral means to pass! But above and beyond this there was another issue: it was who they were or, at least, what they represented themselves to be - religious Jews - acting in a reprehensible manner. I had heard that the so-called "Orthodox" disdained non-religious Jews for their lack of observance and assimilationist tendencies - and yet - what sort of models were these two? They made me feel ashamed. I felt I had to say something. I walked over to them. The instructor had not yet arrived. I pointed at them. "What you guys are doing is disgusting!" I said with clenched teeth. But if I thought their consciences were going to be bothered, I was dead wrong. They merely dismissed me with a wave of their hands and a laugh, telling me to mind my own business.

I felt there was little I could do so I held in my anger and returned to my seat. All I could think about at that moment were the unkind stories I had heard about "people with black hats and long beards who are crooks." Once again the image of "religion" was somewhat diminished for me. Had that been the end of the incident, it might have helped to influence my life in a direction other than the one it ultimately took. Happily, something else occurred which struck the balance.

The next autumn, I was taking a course in a Liberal Arts elective at CCNY. Sitting next to me in class was a young man named David Gefreiter. I will never forget him or the lesson he taught me. David was a student at a right-wing Orthodox yeshiva. We became friendly during the semester, and I often asked him questions dealing with Jewish philosophy. He listened very patiently and tried his best to answer. I remember him as a young man with a lot of humility and a good-natured smile. One evening, during the course of our conversation, I mentioned the incident with the two "young men with yarmulkes" who had cheated on the test, and asked him what was so great about being "religious" if one could "shake and pray" one day, and cheat on an exam the next. I think I almost expected David to come up with some kind of rationalization in their defense, but he surprised me. Frowning, he asked me very softly, "Do you know why their action was reprehensible?" "They were cheating," I said. "It's more than just cheating," he responded, "It's thievery; it's something we call *gneyvas daas* stealing the mind."

"What do you mean?" I asked.

"They were 'stealing' the instructor's mind by misleading him into thinking they knew the material he had taught."

This was a novel concept to me but David was not finished, and what he added impressed me even more. "But they did something much worse," he continued, "By advertising their religiosity in wearing yarmulkes, and acting in this manner, they desecrated the name of God because both the non-Jew and the non-religious Jew will say that these are the *Torah*'s representatives who act like thieves and drive people away from God." And he concluded, "People like those two prevent the coming of the Messiah."

I developed a great respect for David, and I learned much from him. In essence, he told me that the *Torah* attempts to raise Jews to a level of holiness but unfortunately, some of its visible representatives do not comprehend its message, and because of them the religious community at large is diminished. Nevertheless, the *Torah* is not diminished. It remains pure as God's guide to Jewish living, and the actions of a few contemptible individuals can never invalidate it, or afford an excuse for Jews not to try to live up to what it commands.

Part IV

Hear O Israel, *HaShem* our God, *HaShem* is one.

Deuteronomy 6:4

For the commandment which I command thee this day, it is not hidden from thee, neither is it far off. It is not in heaven, that thou shouldst say, Who shall go up for us to heaven, and bring it unto us, that we may hear it and do it? Neither is it beyond the sea, that thou shouldst say, Who shall go over the sea for us, and bring it unto us, that we may hear it and do it? But the word is very nigh unto thee; in thy mouth and in thy heart, that thou mayest do it.

Deuteronomy 30:11-14

The Eternal God is thy refuge, and underneath are the everlasting arms .... Happy art thou, O Israel: who is like unto thee, O people saved by *HaShem*, the shield of thy help, and Who is the sword of thy Excellency! And thine enemies shall be found liars unto thee; and thou shalt tread upon their high places.

Deuteronomy 33:27, 29

The wise son asks: What are the testimonies and the decrees and the laws which *HaShem* our God commanded you?

Passover Haggadah

XXXI
YOUR PEOPLE
SHALL BE
MY PEOPLE

As 1968 drew to a close, I began to evaluate myself as a Jew. My belief in God had reawakened, but on a day-to-day basis I was not living according to the rhythm of the Jewish calendar. Several months earlier, I had told Mike Kahan's brother (who, like Mike, had also recently become observant) that I considered myself a good Jew. As evidence, I said that I was intensely Zionistic and that I observed the Ten Commandments after my own fashion. He replied that I probably was a good person but that he didn't know whether or not I was a good Jew. After all, he knew many non-Jewish Zionists and, he pointed out, Christians also observed the Ten Commandments after a fashion. How, he wanted to know, did I differ from them? I had no answer.

To complicate matters, I was then dating a non-Jewish woman, and the relationship had become serious enough that we were talking about marriage. On many occasions I discussed the importance of my Jewishness with her and told her how the Six Day War, among other events, had evoked a religious yearning in me. I also told her that I wanted my children to be Jewish and that Jewish religious status is dependent on maternal descent.

Although Pamela knew little about Judaism, she was willing to investigate what it had to offer. Perhaps one reason was her own need for some religious structure. She had received none from her parents whom she had described as "nominal Unitarians." Neither of us wished our children to go through the religious perplexity each of us had experienced as youngsters.

For my own part, I wanted to spare my children the difficult search for self-identity. More positively, I wanted them to know early in life that they were members of the Chosen People, bearers of a rich, proud, five-thousand-year old tradition, sons and daughters of the Covenant with God. As yet, however, I myself was not living up to that Covenant.

Pamela told me that raising a family within a religious framework was more appealing to her than the contemporary "do your own thing" concept of child-rearing. How could a child know what his or her own "thing" was without some frame of reference? She said her parents had always told her that she could choose whatever lifestyle suited her, but that meant giving her too much to choose from. Then she added, "If our children want to rebel, at least let them have something to rebel against."

I myself wanted to begin doing something practical on a daily basis, to "act Jewish" - practical, yet simple enough so as not to be overwhelming. I was like a baby sticking a toe in the water.

Then an idea struck me. One of the first practices I had learned in Hebrew school was reciting *berachot*, blessings, specifically those blessings to be said before eating. What could be simpler and less demanding? By pronouncing a benediction before eating a piece of bread, I accomplished two things: I ritualized the act of eating in a Jewish context, and I opened communication with God for the first time in more than a decade. I must admit that it felt strange, even embarrassing at first, but I stuck to it, and after a short while, it began to feel comfortable. I also decided that from then on I would no longer eat shellfish or pork, both of which are forbidden under Jewish law. I even considered attending services, but my lack of real direction and the unpleasant memories associated with synagogues made me hesitate.

Meanwhile, Pamela visited some of the neighborhood synagogues. She discussed her situation with several rabbis and began reading about Judaism. She first arranged a meeting with a local Reform rabbi who was very cordial to her. But the gist of his message was that a gentile had only to "feel Jewish" or to "have a Jewish heart" or to have a "Jewish sense of destiny" to qualify for conversion; he or she need not make a commitment to real change in his or her life. It left Pamela cold. She had intuited what Mike Kahan's brother had told me; there must be more to being a Jew than joining a Zionist organization and being a good person, or "following the Ten Commandments after a fashion."

Even as a gentile, Pamela always had a fondness for Israel, and respect for the Ten Commandments. No, there must be more to it than that, she felt. If she were to become a Jew and a Jewish mother, she did not wish merely to have a Jewish heart; she wanted to become deeply involved with committed Jews.

Pamela next decided to talk to a rabbi at another nearby synagogue. She called to tell me that after a brief interview with him, he had referred her to the rabbi in charge of conversions at the Jewish Theological Seminary.

Meanwhile, I was beginning to feel pangs of guilt about Pam's conversion. What right, I asked myself, had I to ask or expect her to change her whole life just to please me? How could I ask her to expose herself to the extreme difficulties of being Jewish? When a person converts to Judaism, it can result in the severing of all ties with family and friends. Abraham Carmel had told me "there was a gulf" separating him from his family because of his conversion. The residue of latent anti-Semitism in the gentile world cannot be underestimated, and the convert joins a community that has many enemies who will harass, and may even be violent. Converts also place themselves in a position where some Jews may continue to look upon them as outsiders.

These thoughts gave me no rest. I loved Pam and wanted her love; yet to ask her to convert was demanding too much.

I saw Pamela several days before she was scheduled to meet the rabbi at the Jewish Theological Seminary. Painfully, I explained the turmoil within me. I asked her to think carefully, to reconsider, to spare herself the burden of obligation that conversion to Judaism entails. She objected vehemently, saying that words almost failed her because she was under the impression that the matter had been settled, and that she did not want to pursue such a negative line of discussion any further. My state of unease got the better of me, and I did what I considered the "manly" thing to do. I suggested that we stop seeing each other, allow for a cooling off period, and do some hard thinking about the realities of the situation. I myself was not a committed Jew, I said with finality; the *chutspah*, audacity, of even suggesting that Pam undergo a religious conversion was too overwhelming for me. We were both in tears as Pam tried to reason with me while I adamantly refused to listen. We parted. It hurt very much. I kept trying to convince myself that it was for the best.

We agreed to stop seeing each other as a "trial." A month passed. I believed that I would never see Pam again but I wanted to make our parting more definite. I knew that I would not be able to face her and maintain my composure, so I decided to write a farewell letter I was hurt as well as frustrated by the situation, and practically paranoid. I began to feel that somehow it was all her fault that she wasn't Jewish. My letter spoke of the necessity of our being separated from each other for good. I clumsily poured out my feelings which were peppered with harsh accusations, some eight pages worth. Actually, what I had meant to get across was that my children must be Jewish because this was the only way that Jewish continuity could be insured.

Several days after mailing the letter, I received a phone call from Pamela, demanding that we get together immediately to discuss what I had written.

When we met, she told me that she had also believed we would never see each other again but that she was surprised and hurt by my letter which seemed to indict her!

She spoke. I listened. When she was almost finished, she said something that amazed me and changed our lives. She told me that she had been reading and reflecting a great deal about Judaism, that she had visited the rabbi at the Jewish Theological Seminary several times, and that she had discussed conversion with a number of other people as well. Pamela ended by telling me that even if we were never to see each other again she had decided to become a Jew.

I was practically speechless! I mumbled something about having to go home and think things over.

Several days later I called Pamela, invited her to go out, and over a candlelight dinner, asked her to marry me.

XXXII
I START
ATTENDING
TEMPLE SERVICES

One day in February, 1969, Pamela, now my finance, told me she had attended a Friday night service at a synagogue I shall call the Temple for Progressive Judaism. She said that the cantor's renditions were beautifully moving and that the rabbi impressed her. She asked me to accompany her the following Friday evening.

I had not been inside a synagogue for over ten years, and as I prepared to go with Pamela that Friday night, I felt anxious but excited. I was going into a house of God, God with whom I had been out of touch for so long.

Yet, I would not be alone. Pamela would be with me. She had already been attending services there for several weeks, and that night she introduced me to the rabbi. He seemed polite enough, but there was something distant about him. Instead of giving me a warm welcome when we shook hands, he merely remarked that he had surmised that this young woman proselyte must have a Jewish boyfriend or fiancé. This seemed to imply that Pamela's motivation was not primarily religious. Nevertheless, we began to attend Friday night services there regularly. At the time, I knew little about the Temple for Progressive Judaism. I immediately found out that all the prayers were in Hebrew, and I liked that. But I was puzzled by the low attendance. There was never a *minyan* of ten men on Friday evening, even though services were scheduled for six o'clock to allow enough time for working people to attend.

However, as Pam pointed out, the elderly cantor did have a truly sweet voice, and the feeling he put into his *davening*, recital of the prayers, was inspiring. I began familiarizing myself with liturgical Hebrew. Reciting blessings over food had established a pattern of communication with God. Attending services at a temple placed that communication in a group context. I was, for the first time in over a decade, praying with other Jews, even though it was not within a *minyan*. After several weeks, we began to attend Saturday morning services as well.

Friday night had always been a dating night for Pamela and me. One week, Pam said it seemed incongruous to go to a movie after coming out of services. She thought that it somehow "broke" the Sabbath atmosphere. From then on, we went to her apartment or to mine for a Sabbath meal after evening services. Soon we did this on Saturday afternoons as well.

While preparing for her conversion at the Jewish Theological Seminary, Pamela seemed to take the lead in our mutual religious growth. She told me that since she intended to maintain a kosher kitchen once we married, it seemed inconsistent to eat non-kosher food outside of the home. Soon we only went to kosher restaurants when we went out.

Attending services at the Temple for Progressive Judaism was refreshing those first few months. We met other couples and made friends; Pam joined the choir and looked forward to singing each Saturday morning. But slowly, problems of a religious nature began to develop.

To begin with, the majority of the congregants did not keep what I considered to be basic religious practices. Most of them did not eat only kosher food, and if they put anything into maintaining a Sabbath atmosphere beyond temple attendance, it was not obvious to me. This lackadaisical attitude toward observance, I saw, developed out of the complete absence of learning on a congregational level. Without any study groups, Bible or Talmud classes, and with no desire on the members' parts to begin them, religious growth was impossible. The roots of apathy toward observance, I felt, were found in the bland theology of the Temple for Progressive Judaism, according to which the Bible was not to be taken literally, and God was some vague impersonal, beneficent concept. Moreover, it followed from this that the Choosiness of the Jewish people was denied; and if the Temple for Progressive Judaism taught that Jews had not been chosen by God to observe His commandments, then there need be no absolute commitment to do so. In reference to this denial of the tenet of choseness on the part of the Temple for Progressive Judaism, my friend Alan Braum had once remarked, "This is their most serious failing. Any Jew who does not believe that he is a member of the Chosen People has lost the power to effectively pass on the flame of Judaism to the next generation."

The more I discovered about the theology and practice at this synagogue, the more dissatisfied I became. Consider, for example, the way the temple observed Tisha B'Av, the ninth day of the Hebrew month of Av, which commemorates the destruction of Jerusalem and its Temple by both the Babylonians and Romans. Traditional Jews observe Tisha B'Av as a day of mourning. One does not shave or wear leather shoes, which are regarded as signs of ease and well-being. The lights of the synagogue are dimmed, and the worshippers sit on the floor or on special low "mourning" seats. When Pam and I entered the temple on the eve of Tisha B'Av, we were both wearing sneakers and sat on the floor. No one said anything to us but all eyes were upon us. We were the only ones present following the traditional signs of mourning for the Holy Temple of Jerusalem. I felt a bit uneasy. It reminded me of that feeling I had experienced more than ten years earlier in a synagogue when I had been told that I didn't "look right."

Finally, the rabbi arrived. He noticed us and although he didn't say anything to us, I felt that his sermon that evening spoke about us. He told the congregation that our ancestors had always felt great sadness on this most dark day, and that they had responded with displays of self-abasement and contrition. Traditional Jews, he said, had for the past two millennia, worn non-leather shoes on Tisha B'Av and had refused to sit on chairs, preferring the hard, cold floor, as mourners do, during the week of shiva. Of course, he added, his congregants were progressive Jews and hence, wouldn't practice any such outmoded behavior. Incredibly, he was either predicting or limiting the depth of their Jewish observance or both, although they were seeing traditional Tisha B'Av behavior every time they glanced over at Pam and me. I felt that I had been embarrassed and humiliated. We had been ignored and isolated, and, at the same time, insulted. We had not been created as members of the House of Israel which "weepeth sore in the night, and her tears are on her cheeks; among all her lovers she hath none to comfort her." (Lamentations 1:2)

We were solitary mourners caught in an approach to Judaism that was too "sophisticated" and "advanced" for us. We could not, in this environment, develop a deep relationship with a personal God. As stated, their "progressive" view is that God is an impersonal force of goodness (!) in the universe, and one does not pour out one's heart on Tisha B'Av, or at any other time, and beseech Him to rebuild His Holy Temple. How could we, sitting properly in a straight-back chair, and saying prayers to a "force", develop a love relationship with such a God? The widow, the orphan and the stranger wish to cry out. We were representative of the simple, non-intellectual Jew who hopes for the same loving relationship with his God that his ancestors experienced. But this rabbi and his brethren said that they shouldn't have it.

XXXIII
DISENCHANTMENT

When the cantor at the Temple for Progressive Judaism retired, a young man was appointed. He and his wife took an interest in us, and the four of us became friends. But not once did either the rabbi or his wife express an inclination even to talk with us, let alone give us any religious guidance. As a matter of fact, I think it is accurate to say that we were completely ignored by them and that we were never made truly welcome. Why? I don't know.

Since this rabbi obviously could not be the religious guide I needed, I decided to look elsewhere. But Pamela was reluctant. She was ready to overlook the rabbi's coldness. Pamela felt we had friends here and she enjoyed singing in the choir. Why abandon this congregation? Why not try to work for effective change from within? But I felt there could be no change. After all, we were relative newcomers, and any changes we tried to bring about would be viewed as meddlesome by the rabbi.

Because I was now developing a need for a more significant religious experience faster than Pam was, tensions developed between us. The more hostile I became toward the temple and its rabbi, the more she felt obligated to defend both. Admittedly, she had done the initial "leg work." While I had sat around *dreaming* about Judaism, she actively initiated our first contact with a Jewish institution. After a while I realized that arguing with her about the situation was useless. I decided to investigate other synagogues on my own without putting pressure on her to follow me.

For several weeks thereafter I *"shul*-hopped," that is, I attended services at several Conservative and Orthodox synagogues in the area. But I sensed the same lack of feeling I had found in *shuls* before. Not once in any of these synagogues was I approached and wished a *"gut shabbes."* No one paid any attention to me. On one occasion I tried approaching a group of people and saying "hello," but I was only eyed with suspicion and hostility for my "familiarity." There was no warmth, no concern, no reaching out. No one, including the rabbi, was concerned with a stranger like me. This, in my mind, was, and still is, the greatest of shortcomings of twentieth-century American Jewish religious institutions. And not only was there indifference from the congregants, but the very services struck me as sterile and uninspiring. Synagogues like these do nothing to reach out to isolated and unaffiliated Jews.

Discouraged. I returned to the Temple for Progressive Judaism. At least there I knew people who were friendly to me. But the friendliness was not enough to offset the weak theology and the lack of concern with observance.

While attending the Temple for Progressive Judaism's services, I had learned the basic structure of Jewish prayer, but praying to an impersonal "force" was not very satisfying. This was not the Judaism I remembered seeing and feeling as a child in my grandfather's *shtibl*. Moreover, although the rabbi remained indifferent to me, his sermons, his manner of speech, everything about him, seemed to antagonize me more and more.

One evening, Pam and I attended a panel discussion at the temple on "Jewish Youth: Prospective for the 1970s. At the end of the discussion, the rabbi took questions from the audience. A young woman stood up and said that this was the first time she had been in a "Jewish place of worship" in years. She said that the attitudes and behavior of people in *shuls* had always turned her off; and yet, she added, she knew that Judaism had beautiful things to say. Why, she wanted to know, did "religious people" not act in accordance with what the *Torah* demanded, *chesed v'emet* (loving kindness and truth?

The rabbi smugly responded that she had no right to pass judgment on people in *shuls* since she, by her own admission, was not involved with synagogue life. Dismissing her totally, and avoiding the real question, he was about to take another question.

Bruce Goldman, an activist Reform rabbi during the late 1960's, happened to be in the audience. He leaped to his feet and demanded to know why the rabbi was being so condescending to this interested young woman.

"Excuse me Bruce," the rabbi said, "but whenever I see a young girl in a miniskirt in synagogue, I tend to doubt her religious motivation. Usually she's there to meet boys."

The young woman burst into tears at this affront, and we were all shocked. Goldman began shouting, demanding that the rabbi give the young lady the courtesy and respect of answering her question. A loud argument ensued with the rabbi finally demanding: "Oh Bruce, for Christ's sake, keep quiet!"

"He seems to doubt the religious sincerity of anyone who doesn't fit in with his idea of Judaism," I exclaimed to Pamela. "I don't know how much more of this I can take." I was steaming!

Soon after I found out how little I could take. An incident occurred which was the proverbial last straw. It was the Sabbath on which the *sedra, Shemini* Leviticus, 9-11) is read. This section contains the story of the sons of Aaron, the high priest:

> ... each of them took his censer, and put fire therein, and put incense thereon, and offered strange fire before *HaShem,* which He commanded them not. And there went out a fire from *HaShem* and devoured them, and they died before *HaShem.*

After the *Torah*-reading, the rabbi gave an emotional sermon in which he angrily stated that we do not have the right to believe that just because these two well-meaning men, Aaron's sons, died as the result of a chemical explosion, that they had been guilty of any sin, such as bringing strange fires before a wrathful *Jehovah* No! We *modern, advanced* Jews had to give our own interpretation to the story, not the interpretation given by "that piece of garbage in the ark!" and he pointed to the *Torah*.

It was at that moment that I got up, left the temple, and never went back. I told Pamela that she could stay if she was happy there, but she would have to attend without me.

XXXIV
I FIND
OTHER
JEWISH GROUPS

During the late spring of 1969, I became aware of The New York *Havurah* and the Jewish Liberation Project, two counter-culture groups that had recently come into existence. *Havurah* was a kind of free form "synagogue" split off from the Conservative movement, and consisted primarily of people in their twenties who did not feel comfortable in establishment religious institutions. The *Havurah* held Saturday morning services in an apartment on the upper west side of Manhattan, and during the week, conducted study groups in the homes of various members.

The Jewish Liberation Project called itself a Socialist Zionist entity and was founded by former members of various 1960s radical left-wing campus political groups who left when these groups began to exhibit anti-Semitic and anti-Israel tendencies after the Six Day War. Its aims were to work for the "liberation of the Jewish people, both in Israel and in the Diaspora, through a socialist revolution" and to "map out a modern Jewish life style appropriate for the 1970s."

After I decided not to return to the Temple for Progressive Judaism, I began to attend services at the *Havurah* on a weekly basis. Although Pamela preferred to continue going to the Temple for Progressive Judaism, she accompanied me to the *Havurah* on alternate Saturdays. Services at the *Havurah* were informal and unstructured. Each Saturday, from five to twenty men and women would meet at the apartment starting about 10 a.m. Conservative and Orthodox prayer books were used. Sitting in easy chairs, or on the floor, worshippers would begin praying spontaneously, and when *shacharit*, the morning service, was finished, they would hold a *Torah* study session in lieu of reading the *Torah* aloud. Sometimes these study sessions were informal discussions of the weekly reading from the *Torah*; sometimes these were prepared discourses by one of the members. After *Torah* study, we ended either with the regular *mussaf*, additional services, or a programmed "happening," such as a light show, poetry reading or guitar recital. *Kiddush*, the special Sabbath blessing over wine, was then made by one of the regular members.

Pamela and I also attended a study seminar on the *Siddur*, the prayerbook, at the home of Reuven Kimmelman, a *Havurah* member. These seminars were usually restricted to the regular membership, but several members, among them Alan Mintz, Bill Novak, and Reuven Kimmelman personally asked us to attend. Later that year, Alan Mintz submitted my name for membership to the entire group, and as I shall soon relate, I was turned down.

As for my involvement with the Jewish Liberation Project, for a period of several months, Pamela and I regularly attended meetings of the "life-styles" committee of the Project. These sessions took place on Sunday nights at the homes of various members. Unfortunately, they turned out to be some of the most unproductive meetings I have ever attended. For the most part, members spent their time just venting anti-Establishment sentiments or complaining about how the Jews had been betrayed by the Radical Left. Sometimes discussions would deal with various petitions such as one demanding the immediate return of the "West Bank to the Palestinian people," that was to be presented to the "repressive" Israeli government. Some participants who seemed to use these meetings in lieu of therapy sessions, delivered aimless diatribes. Occasionally meetings turned into screaming matches which became contests to see who could yell "unfair" the loudest and longest.

Whenever Pamela and I tried to bring a meeting back to "lifestyles" proposals, we were either shouted down or ignored, especially since most of our suggestions dealt with religious issues. It soon became apparent that socialism and politics were the only concerns of the group and noisy arguments its main activity. At one meeting, several of the members were denouncing the "restrictive land-grabbing Israeli government." Pamela and I protested. "Idiots!", I exclaimed. There aren't enough anti-Semites in the world among the non-Jews? You have to join their ranks?" We walked out of the meeting. So much for our involvement in "Jewish liberation."

The *Havurah* experience was also less than satisfactory for me. Though a newcomer, I had the *chutspah* to criticize some of their practices, such as playing music on *Shabbat* and using non-kosher wine for *kiddush*. My outspokenness obviously annoyed many. When Alan Mintz submitted my name for membership, I was voted down by an overwhelming majority.

It was at this point that I stopped attending services at the *Havurah* although I continued going to the classes at Reuven Kimmelman's home.

By the summer of 1969, I had no further desire to attend synagogue services, or even to continue any Jewish studies. Pamela still attended the Temple for Progressive Judaism services, but she was no longer happy about going. I was disgusted with all the Jewish groups I had come to know, and Pamela wasn't happy with her affiliations. Thinking back, the possibility exists that I would have abandoned my search for a meaningful religious Judaism at that point, had I not received a suggestion from an entirely unexpected source.

XXXV
I HEAR ABOUT LINCOLN SQUARE SYNAGOGUE

Pamela worked for a Jewish dentist, a man in his sixties, with three marvelous qualities: a sense of humor, the "patience of Job," and a sympathetic ear. I cannot count the times I sat in his dentist's chair, ranting and raving about the deficiencies of the Jewish religious establishment while Pamela stifled her embarrassment and quietly expressed her own frustration and disappointment.

One day, Pamela's boss responded by suggesting that we visit a synagogue on 66th Street and West End Avenue; he said it was led by an intelligent and sensitive young rabbi. He said his nephew had been the original *baal-kore*, reader of the *Torah*, there and had nothing but good things to say about it. That *Shabbat* the weather was mild, and Pamela suggested we walk down. I had my doubts, but she pointed out that we had nothing to lose. I agreed to give it a try.

From my very first contact with the Lincoln Square Synagogue and its rabbi, Shlomo Riskin, I knew that this was like no *shul* I had ever been in before. The atmosphere radiated the warmth, friendliness and concern for the entire Jewish community that I had been seeking for so long. And I felt electricity in the air. I had not experienced such religious excitement since my initial experience with Hebrew-Christianity (a sad commentary on the Jewish religious institutions I had attended).

At the time, the synagogue was a renovated ground floor apartment that quickly filled to overflowing on *Shabbat* mornings. I immediately recognized Rabbi Riskin as the dynamic and eloquent speaker I had heard at the Soviet Jewry rally five years earlier. Rabbi Riskin would walk out among the congregants as he taught *Torah* and look directly into their eyes as though he were personally teaching and reaching out to each and every one. A man sitting next to me smiled and said with unconcealed pride, "Our rabbi! A short man, but such a tall *neshome*, soul." I could hardly contain myself and gestured to Pamela across the *mechitsah*, the separation between men and women. I could tell she agreed with me.

After services, we introduced ourselves to Rabbi Riskin, who was anxious to greet and know every newcomer. He welcomed us warmly and urged us to please return as often as possible. I explained to him that we were not Orthodox. His response was that his *shul* was for all Jews. Obviously, here was a place of Jewish worship, which, though Orthodox by orientation, did not require a Jew to carry a card verifying "strictly glat, without imperfection." One did not have to "look right" to be welcome.

Shortly thereafter, Pamela and I began to attend Lincoln Square Synagogue regularly, learning *Torah* and *mitsvos*, commandments, in a meaningful way. Rabbi Riskin's patience and compassion were impressive.

He always had time for questions and special problems; no question was too "stupid" and no problem too insignificant for his consideration. Above all, his humility and love of Jews were over powering. In my estimation, he fulfilled the rabbinical precepts in *Pirke Avot*, Ethics of the Fathers:

> Be of the disciples of Aaron; love peace, pursue peace, love God's creatures, and draw them near to the *Torah*.
>
> *Hillel (1:12)*

> Let the honor of him whom you teach be as dear to you as your own honor.
>
> *Elazar ben Shammua (4:15)*

XXXVI

WE ASK RABBI RISKIN TO PERFORM OUR MARRIAGE

Pam and I set an August date for our wedding. Since I had been so impressed by Rabbi Riskin, I wanted him to perform the ceremony. I discussed this with Pamela and she agreed. We met with him to discuss our wedding, and told him we would be honored if he would perform the ceremony. Rabbi Riskin knew that Pamela was planning to convert and asked us under whose auspices her conversion was to take place. We answered that it was being handled by Rabbi Alstat of the Jewish Theological Seminary. Rabbi Riskin became reflective and then said, "I am willing to officiate at your wedding, but it would require my handling Pamela's conversion to insure that it is done properly." Perplexed, we asked him what he meant, and he proceeded to explain how important it was for the conversion to be acceptable to *all* Jews. Rabbi Riskin then mentioned a young man from a yeshiva background who was preparing to marry. He and his fiancée, who had recently become observant, were devoted to one another. And they were both committed to following a traditional Jewish life-style. The young man had introduced his fiancée to Rabbi Riskin, who was quite impressed with her. Arrangements for the wedding proceeded when it came to light that the young woman's maternal grandmother had undergone a non-Orthodox conversion. Because the grandmother's conversion lacked the *halachic* requirements of both ritual immersion as well as the grandmother's acceptance of the commandments (as interpreted by historical Talmudic authority), the Jewishness of the grandmother could not be authenticated, and was therefore not universally recognized within the Jewish community. What were the implications of this? They were staggering for that young couple! In effect, since the grandmother was not considered by some to be Jewish, neither was the mother nor the daughter. Furthermore, the young woman's maternal uncles, aunts, and cousins by blood were similarly affected. "One can well imagine," Rabbi Riskin said, "the severe trauma suffered by all involved. This is just one incident." Rabbi Riskin continued, "There are many others. That is why although I feel compassion for people caught in such unfortunate circumstances; I have always advocated that divorce and conversion remain strictly under Orthodox auspices."

After discussing this with us a while longer, Rabbi Riskin asked Pam, "Are you willing to refrain from turning lights on and off on the Sabbath?"

Pamela thought for a minute and responded, "I'm not sure I can promise that." Needless to say, it was not the lights per se that concerned the rabbi, but that they were a barometer of Pam's commitment, at that time, to Jewish observance.

Rabbi Riskin shook his head. "You see," he added, "that young woman who wanted to marry the yeshiva student was willing to keep the Sabbath in all of its details. She accepted historical rabbinic authority and wanted to live in accordance with Jewish law. Her conversion would not have been questioned by any one."

It was clear that not much could be said after that, and that our meeting was at an end. As we were leaving, Rabbi Riskin spoke conciliating to Pam. "Come back to see me in a year if you decide that it is possible for you to adhere to the Jewish practices we've discussed."

Pam said to me afterwards, "I respect Rabbi Riskin for his honesty and concern. I'm going to write to him and thank him for leveling with me." That was the beginning of what was to become a two year correspondence between my wife and the rabbi. It led to a growing mutual respect.

Pam and I decided that the only alternative left was to ask Rabbi Alstat to perform the wedding. The ceremony took place that August, at Temple *Anshe Chesed*, on the first day of the week during which the *Torah* section Ki *Teytsey* is read.

XXXVII
REACTIONS TO BECOMING OBSERVANT

Over the years, I have had numerous discussions with *baalei-tshuvah* on what led them to acceptance of a *Torah* lifestyle, and how their families and friends reacted. Usually, they encountered opposition, even overt displeasure. I consider this reaction to be part of a general opposition to religion by disaffiliated Jews. For the most part the *baalei-tshuvah,* I am referring to are young people still living at home with parents or very recently living on their own. Sometimes this lack of family acceptance continues even after the *baal-tshuvah* marries.

Fortunately, my family did not oppose me as I became more observant. Many factors account for this, particularly my previous experience with the missionaries and my subsequent phase of militant atheism. My family had learned to become increasingly tolerant of my changes. Besides, I had been living on my own for nearly a decade, and my growing observance didn't really inconvenience any of them. My mother, in fact, encouraged me. This is understandable considering that she was a woman raised in an Orthodox milieu in an Eastern European *shtetl.* After she came to this country and married, my mother still retained some religious practices such as keeping a kosher kitchen and lighting candles on Friday evenings.

My family understood that my marriage to a convert necessarily motivated me toward reexamining my life style. I had first introduced Pam to my family some four or five months before we decided to marry. When I told my mother our plans, she looked at me with grave concern, and quietly but intensely asked, "Is she going to accept your Jewishness?" I explained that Pam was preparing to convert. Pamela and I discussed our plans to establish a religious household, with my mother, and any opposition she may have harbored toward our marriage disappeared. Thereafter, my mother and Pamela developed a closeness that was never broken, and which manifested itself in many tender and endearing ways. Pamela's family raised no objections and this was not surprising since her brother's wife is Jewish by birth. Pam's brother had undergone a Reform Jewish conversion.

To my surprise, it was friends who voiced the strongest opposition to my becoming a *baal-tshuvah,* especially those who were non-religious Jews. I could not fathom the depth of the antipathy and resentment my observances aroused in them. But clearly it pained them. As a result, I became more involved with new friends who shared my Jewish values.

Shortly after our wedding. Pamela perceptively commented: "A time will come when our old friends will no longer want to associate with us nor we with them." Truthfully, I did not agree with her and said so. After all. I argued, I had managed to retain relationships with others when I became involved with the Hebrew Christians, so why should my involvement with Judaism alienate close friends, some of whom were themselves Jews? Pamela replied knowingly, "You will continue to change but they will not, and finally they will not be able to understand you at all. They will then blame you for drifting away." I could not believe that I would change to the extent that relationships which had remained close for so many years would quickly be terminated by something as positive as my involvement in Judaism. But Pam said, "Wait and see; it will happen." Ultimately, her words proved to be prophetic.

XXXVIII
ENCOUNTERS WITH *LUBOVITCHER* HASIDIM

Not long after I was married, I came in contact with another group of Jews, the Lubovitcher (Chadbad"*) *Hasidim,* who also showed me the meaning of *ahavat Yisrael,* love of the Jewish people. My first encounter with them occurred in the spring of 1970. Nearly a year earlier, Pamela had expressed admiration for the *Hasidim.* Their extreme visibility and complete *Torah* commitment exemplified the ideal of the Jew par excellence. Here were no mere Sabbath Jews but people who lived full *Torah* lives every minute of each day and who, because of their conspicuous dress, were often the first to give up their lives whenever waves of hatred and persecution fell upon the Jewish people in Europe.

*Chabad is an acronym standing for the Divine (and correspondingly human) attributes through which God can be comprehended, according to *Lubovitch* philosophy, namely: *Chochmh* - wisdom. *Binah* - understanding, and *Daat* - knowledge.

The *Lubovitcher Hasidim* especially appealed to us as "disciples of Aaron," drawing *HaShem's* creatures closer to the *Torah.*

During my senior year (1970) at City College of New York, I joined the Jewish Students' League on campus; it was through the League that I learned about the *Chabad* on-campus study program in Chumash, Bible, and *Gemarah,* Talmud, which was open to all Jewish students. Each class met once a week and I eagerly looked forward not only to the formal learning experience of Bible and Talmud, but also to the informal learning experience of *Chabad ahavat Yisrael,* love of Israel, as well. It was a perfect complement to what I was experiencing at Lincoln Square Synagogue.

The *Chabadniks* completely destroyed the hateful secular Jewish stereotype that the *Hasidim* consider all non-religious Jews *goyim.* They certainly did not! One of the young men with whom I was learning said to me, "We are willing to approach countless thousands of unlearned Jews in order to gain just one *yidishe neshome,* Jewish soul, and when we mekarev, bring that one closer, we feel that we have been successful."

"Why," I asked, "do you take the trouble to go out of your way to seek out the assimilated ones which the other so-called religious Jews had already given up for lost?"

I was told that one of the greatest *mitsvos,* commandments, for Jews is to ransom fellow Jews who had been kidnapped. "Jews who come from families in which the chain of tradition has been broken, are being held for ransom by their ignorance and by the *yetser hara*, evil inclination," they explained. "It is as if they had been kidnapped while they were babies and brought up as gentiles. In fact, our tradition calls such a one, *tinok shenishba*, a stolen baby. It is our Jewish duty to rescue them from the 'other side.'"

"But," I said, "take me, for example. Being a religious Jew is not an easy matter. I have really only begun to do mitsvos, and I seriously doubt that I will ever be able to obey all the commandments."

"Of course you won't," they replied. "Even we, who have been religious all our lives, do not perform all the mitsvos. We read in *Pirke Avot* (2:21) that Rabbi Tarfon used to say, 'You are not called upon to complete the work, yet you are not free to desist from it.'."

I realized that here was an essential difference in attitude between Judaism and Christianity, a difference between the basic pessimism of the latter, and the inherent optimism of the former.

In Galatians 5:3, Paul the apostle wrote to the gentiles that those who accepted the *Torah* were "debtors to the whole Law," implying that failure to live up to even a single commandment nullified the observance of all the others, and was sufficient to condemn an individual. Judaism, on the other hand, sees the individual's responsibility to the mitsvos as part of a larger responsibility, - to the community or nation. Fulfilling all of the *Torah's* commandments is a national Jewish responsibility. Unlike Paul and subsequent Christians, we Jews do not feel that failure to live up to every single commandment either signifies the nullification of the entire *Torah*, or cancels our obligation to observe what we can. It was not given to us either to "complete the work" or "desist from it." Our *kavannah*, or intention, was sufficient to earn us *HaShem's* grace. And we, not Christians, were the first to proclaim that grace. The New Testament accuses us of boasting that we are justified before God by performing mitsvos. This accusation is implicit in Luke 18:9-14, Romans 3:20,28, and explicit in Galatians 2:16. One has but to read through the book of Deuteronomy to see that such an imputation is untrue. In Deuteronomy, we find the reasons why we are to keep the mitsvos; namely, to possess the land that *HaShem* has given us (4:1, 11:8), to gain length of days (4:40, 5:33, 6:24, 11:9, 22.7), for the well being of ourselves and our children (5:29, 29:9), to be aware of *HaShem's* love (8:5), for humility (24:18, 22), and to be a holy people (26:19). Nowhere did we ever claim to fulfill the commandments in order to be "justified." Following the *Torah* was our *simchah*, joy. And in *Pirke Avot*, we find the words of Antigonus of Sokho (1:3), "Be not like servants who serve the Master for the sake of receiving a reward, but be like servants who serve the Master without the expectation of receiving a reward, and let the fear of Heaven be upon you."

I kept in touch with the *Chabad Hasidim* after my graduation from college. In 1971, Pamela and I were invited to spend a weekend in the Crown Heights section of Brooklyn during a *Chabad pegishah*, or encounter, for young couples. It was an unforgettable experience.

We arrived on Friday afternoon at the *Chabad* House to the sounds of lively Hasidic music being played over a public address system. People, some in suits and dresses, others in jeans and sandals, were standing around waiting to be directed to the particular Lubovitch family at whose home they would be sleeping.

That weekend, we all ate together, sang together, prayed together, questioned together, and learned together. Our hosts showed kindness, patience and understanding of the diverse backgrounds from which we had come to encounter *Yiddishkeit*, Jewishness. When one young man remarked that he had recited more blessings that *Shabbat* than he had ever said during his entire life, one of the *Hasidim* good naturedly remarked that perhaps he should say a blessing for that as well.

On *Shabbat* morning, wrapped in a large prayer shawl. I allowed myself to be transported in prayer to a deep level of feeling and understanding. Pam smilingly remarked to me later that day that she had been watching me and that my "religious batteries were really charged." I laughed, but it was true.

On the last day of the *pegishah*, I asked one of the *Chabadniks* whether someone could come to my home and teach me how to put on *tefillin*, phylacteries, which I had unsuccessfully tried to teach myself to do. These, coincidentally, were *Lubovitch tefillin*. That I had unsuccessfully tried to teach myself. These *Lubovitch tefillin* I had acquired in an unexpected manner some months before. One evening at a Purim party given by the Jewish Liberation Project, a young man, Bob Neiss, told me that he had begun to practice the *mitsvah of tefillin* I told him that I had also been thinking of getting *tefillin*. A few days later, Bob called and said that he had a set for me. Taken aback, I asked him how he had obtained them. He said that the day after the party he met some *Lubovitcher Hasidim* and mentioned that someone he knew was interested in beginning the *mitsvah* of *tefillin* Right on the spot, one of the *Hasidim* handed him a pair of *tefillin* and asked him to give them to me!

Over the years, Pamela and I have spent many *Shabbatot* in the Lubovitch community, and have formed numerous friendships. The willingness of the *Chabad Hasidim* to assist us when we requested help, no matter how great the need, has deeply impressed me. Several days after the *pegishah*, I received a call from a Hasid in Newark, New Jersey, who said he would gladly come to my home to teach me how to put on the *tefillin*. To this very day, I regularly don those same *Lubovitch tefillin*.

XXXIX

A GROWING COMMITMENT TO JEWISH LAW

By 1971, we had been involved with the Lincoln Square Synagogue community for nearly two years. Our level of learning and observance was steadily increasing under the guidance of Rabbi Riskin and his associate, Rabbi Hirschl Cohen.

There we learned to appreciate fully the structure that *halachic* Judaism, that is, Judaism according to the traditional law, offers to the people of Israel. It is a structure that supports those who incorporate it into their daily lives, as King Solomon wrote:

> It is a tree of life to them that lay hold upon it; and happy is every one that retaineth it...
> Its ways are ways of pleasantness, and all its paths are peace.
>
> *Proverbs 3:18, 17*

Moreover, it allows us a glimpse of God's love for the Jewish people down through the ages. As Moses said:

> Know therefore that *HaShem* thy God, He is God, the faithful God, which keepeth covenant and loving kindness with them that love Him and keep His commandments to a thousand generations.
>
> *Deuteronomy, 7:9*

Through Rabbi Riskin and Rabbi Cohen, we learned that only a God who *cares* will *command*. *Hashem* entered into a love relationship with Israel at Sinai, and Israel has shown her love for Him by doing and listening to all that He has commanded. The Sabbath given to the Jewish nation, which the religious nation faithfully keeps, has sustained Jews and given them weekly rest in a world which knows little repose. Every seventh day, the committed Jew declares that things of this world have no mastery over him. He has only one Master, his Father in heaven. As the candles are kindled on Friday night, so the *Lubovitcher Rebbe (shelita)*, "may his life be good and long," " tells us, *light is sown in the world*, a world darkened by insensitivity and the deification of the human ego.

The commandments governing the Jew's attitude and behavior at his table and in his bedroom train him to respect the body and soul that *HaShem* has given him because they are fashioned in God's image.

At Lincoln Square Synagogue, I came to learn that the *Torah* is not simply a book of "Thou shalt not." "It is a love letter to us from a God who wishes us to love Him and show our love for Him by keeping His commandments:

> …upon thy heart, and thou shalt drill them into thy children, and speak of them when thou sittest in thy house and when thou walkest on the road, and when thou retirest and when thou risest up. And thou shalt bind them as a sign upon thy hand, and they shall be as ornaments between thine eyes, they shall be written on the doorposts of thy house and upon thy gates.
>
>

Deuteronomy, 6:4-9

We also learned that God loves the stranger, especially the Jewish stranger, even though he or she doesn't necessarily "look right." Although we still had a long way to go, we had travelled far during the two years since that first Friday night at the Temple for Progressive Judaism. Upon reflection, Pamela said that Rabbi Alstat, the rabbi at the Jewish Theological Seminary, had been kind to her, but he had not inspired her to fully accept Jewish law. She had become observant along with me in a slow, sometimes painful process, assiduously grappling with, accepting, and internalizing one observance after another.

One day Pamela told me that although she "felt Jewish," something was still lacking: the incontrovertibility and incontestability of her Jewishness in the eyes of the total Jewish nation which Rabbi Riskin had spoken to us about. Now she had reached that point at which she would allow a light to remain shining one day out of every week. On a Sunday in May, 1971, my wife again entered the *mikveh;* the traditional Jewish ritularium of purification, and underwent an Orthodox conversion.

XL
REFLECTIONS ON ISRAEL

In the summer of 1971, Pamela and I fulfilled a long-time dream, to visit Israel. Even years before we met, Pam had planned such a trip with her sister to work on a *kibbutz*

Our route was based in part on the people we wanted to see. First stop was Haifa, and then we spent a week in the peaceful atmosphere of Safed. Many of our friends expressed surprise that we would spend that much time in a city most visitors pass through in a matter of hours. After all, it is a spot with relatively few "holy places." But we felt that the idea of visiting "holy places" was more Christian than Jewish. We, as Jews, ought to visit "holy people." That, to me, is a major reason for visiting Israel; we should do so to meet and establish spiritual ties with our fellow Jews. As Rabbi Joseph Singer of Congregation Mt. Sinai of Washington Heights once said, "Too many Jews go to Israel to see places and not enough to see *people!*"

From Safed we travelled south to Jerusalem and Beersheva to visit friends. We also spent a *Shabbat* at. Kedma, an experimental ranch-style *kibbutz* which served as a combination yeshiva, retreat, and training center for young Americans who had been caught up in the drug and hippy scene and were now trying to "find themselves." Run by Reuven and Sarah Mandel, *baalei tshuvah*, Kedma offered what it called "*Torah* Therapy" to any young person willing to submit to a disciplined Orthodox life-style. The Mandels, two strong personalities, had previously been involved in the gambling and drug life-style of Las Vegas. On the particular *Shabbat* we spent at Kedma, the Mandels were hosting a *Shabbat*on for students from an American yeshiva. I found the atmosphere exuberant, and the flamboyant personalities of the Mandels exhilarating.

Two years later I met the Mandels again, this time in the Crown Heights section of Brooklyn at a Lubo-vitcher weekend sponsored by the Hasidim. Due to a number of factors still not quite clear to me, but apparently political and social in nature, Kedma was closed down by the Israeli government, and the Mandels returned to the United States to set up a similar venture somewhere in California. Since our meeting in Brooklyn, however, I have lost track of them.

From Kedma, we returned to Jerusalem for a few days, and then completed our visit with a short stay in Tel Aviv. Anyone who was in Israel during the summer of 1971 can testify to a mood of extreme optimism. Indeed, it was practically euphoric, and emanated both from residents and visitors. It was just four years after the Six Day War, and the Jews of Israel were dreamily unaware of the *Yom Kippur* War to come two years later. They felt that nothing but a glorious future awaited the Jewish State, "the beginning of the flowering of redemption," to quote the prayer book. Even on *Tisha* B'Av, the day commemorating the destruction of the sacred Temples, when the dominant sentiment is one of sadness and introspection, a note of levity was in the air that year. At the Western Wall, the last vestige of the Temple still standing, Pamela and I joined countless thousands of other Jews caught up in the near delirium and jubilation elicited by the zeitgeist.

We soon became aware of others who, like some Jews, also believed that the world was entering the Messianic period. The return of Jews to the Land of Israel, and their subsequent success there, was interpreted by fundamentalist Christians as a sign of the imminent return of their Messiah. This conclusion spurred some of them on in their efforts to convert Jews to Christianity. As a result, Hebrew-Christian groups began to establish missions in the "Holy Land," and to proselytize. Particularly susceptible to the missionaries were immigrants from Russia who felt themselves to be, and who indeed were, cut off from both the authentic religious community and the Israeli religious establishment. For indeed, we sadly discovered that in Israel, as well as in the United States, those Jews who didn't "look right," were not accepted by the Orthodox, and in turn, either through ignorance of the beauty and grandeur of Jewish tradition or through past negative experiences with Orthodox Jews, became negative toward all religious Jews.

After the Six Day War, non-religious Israelis were ripe for outreach. But the Israeli religious leadership failed disgracefully to respond adequately to the soul-searching going on among many Israelis caught up in the miraculous victory. To those who would take exception with me and counter that many *yeshivot* sprang up in Israel to answer the needs of those seeking "roots", it's my impression that these have attracted mainly young American Jews disenfranchised by an intensely materialistic lifestyle in the United States. The overwhelming majority of Israelis of all ages remains unreached and untouched. And the Hebrew-Christian movement was not slow in recognizing that they could appeal to this spiritual hunger in Israel. They proceeded to exploit it with some success.

Just as this laissez-faire attitude toward Israel's non-religious Jews by so-called religious Jews was sad indeed, so the reaction to the justly perceived missionary threat on the part of a certain segment of Israel's religious community was equally disheartening. As we were leaving Safed for Jerusalem, we heard that the police had discovered the murdered body of a Christian missionary on the periphery of the *Mea Shearim* area, an enclave of extreme Orthodox zealots in Jerusalem. Instead of working toward a heightened awareness and determination to compete with the Christian missionaries to save Jewish souls, which I feel could easily have been accomplished; the typical reaction was fear and mindless violence.

Subsequently, some Israeli governmental figures pushed for legislation to forbid active proselytization within the country, a move I support in spite of my favoring religious freedom in the United States. The religious plurality in the United States necessitates strong separation between church and state, but the same is not true in Israel. As my friend, Freda Bluestone-Birnbaum told me, "There are many Christian and Moslem countries, but only one Jewish country and we cannot risk permitting Israel to be up for grabs!" But even if there is legislation in Israel prohibiting active proselytizing, the effect would not be enough. The only real solution, I feel, depends on significant numbers of observant Jews actively working to counteract such missionizing by a positive outreach program. It has yet to occur either in Israel or the United States, and the Jewish community is destroying its future viability by not making a much more vigorous effort.

XLI
A SUITABLE JEWISH ENVIRONMENT

1972 was not a good year for me. In fact, it was a period that tested both my faith and my marriage. This adversity was highlighted all the more because the year commenced with so much promise. There was no indication that anything could go wrong.

I was just finishing my first semester as a graduate student at Hunter College, and Pamela was in her senior year at CCNY. We had recently moved to a larger apartment in the Washington Heights section of Manhattan and early in January we learned that Pamela was pregnant. I was working as a community educator for the State of New York Narcotic Addiction Control Commission, speaking to community groups about the drug problem in New York City, and counseling addicts and their families. It was at this time that an economic recession began leading to mass unemployment. State agencies cut budgets and laid off provisional employees. In March, 1972, I received a letter from Albany informing me that I would be terminated at the end of the month. At the time, I thought that my period of unemployment would not be long. I did not know it would last eleven months, an eternity to me at the time.

By the end of April, it became obvious that we would be depending on unemployment benefits and food stamps for some time to come, so Pamela decided to get a part-time job. With both of us going to school. worrying about making ends meet, trying to adjust to our new Washington Heights community which, while it was friendly and supportive to its old, long established members, as in the case with most Jewish religious communities, was anything but that to new-comers. All this, coupled with my difficulty in finding a job, caused a strain that began to show. As is common in families where the breadwinner loses his job, Pamela and I began to exhibit signs of moodiness and irritability, and spats over trivial issues increased.

One Saturday night toward the end of May, Pamela suffered a miscarriage. After that, a sense of hopelessness overtook us both, and life seemed devoid of meaning to me. I stopped attending synagogue and we reached a point where we even stopped dressing up for *Shabbat*. One day we sat down and spoke to each other about giving up everything, including Judaism and our marriage. We decided to discuss these matters with Rabbi Riskin. Both Pam and I felt an obligation to talk with him since he had been so instrumental in leading us to Orthodoxy, and I supposed he felt a mutual responsibility to us as his "disciples."

Rabbi Riskin met with us and we discussed our problems. Above all, I realized that we had made a mistake in moving from the supportive West Side community of Lincoln Square Synagogue to the Washington Heights area.

Rabbi Riskin spoke to us comfortingly about the loss of the baby and the difficulties we were experiencing. He said that it would be a mistake to let the pressure of events causes us to make any irrational decisions regarding such serious matters as our marriage and religious life. He also suggested that we try to spend Jewish holidays and as many Sabbaths as possible in his community, and he helped us make arrangements to do so, all the while meeting with us regularly and providing supportive counseling.

Fortunately, we had the strength to pull ourselves out of much of the self-pity we were involved in and we came to the conclusion that splitting up was not something we really wanted to do. Regarding Judaism, Pamela said to me one day, "I guess once you know the 'secrets,' it's difficult, if not impossible, to go back to the old life." It was true. The religious life of the past three years had touched us more deeply than we had realized, and when we gave thought to it, even contemplating the possibility of giving it up was like standing at the edge of an abyss and staring down into it.

We continued to spend Sabbaths and holidays at the homes of friends we had made in the Lincoln Square Synagogue community. One day toward the end of 1972, our friends, Arthur and Julie Cronen, called us and said they were going to Florida for a few weeks and asked us whether we would like to stay in their apartment over *Shabbat*. We accepted their offer.

On that Sabbath, I happened to meet a man who owned a building near Lincoln Square Synagogue. He asked me whether I was a member of the shul and if so, why he had never seen me at services. I explained to him that we did not live in the neighborhood but were anxious to move back. He told me to call him after the Sabbath and he would see what he could do. I contacted him and he said an apartment with a reasonable rent was going to become available in his building.

In February, 1973, we moved back to the Upper West Side. A week later I was hired as a counselor for a drug addiction rehabilitation program.

Moving away from the West Side made me aware of how important it is to live in a Jewish environment that will support one's religious development and also be compatible with one's particular temperament and personality. Because I was just beginning to feel my way into Orthodox Judaism when I moved to Washington Heights, I did not have sufficient strength to maintain my commitment. I missed the warmth of the Lincoln Square community. Now I realize that my failure to adapt to a new neighborhood rested as much with me as with the particular area to which I had moved. But I understand that for a Jewish *neshome*, soul, to flourish, it must be nurtured in an environment in which there are caring Jews.

This is a problem that confronts many Jews who are seeking to intensify their commitment. To maintain one's Orthodoxy, a Jew must live in a proper *Torah* environment, that is, proper for *him*, and this is not very easy to achieve. It does not mean that someone else might not have succeeded in an environment where I couldn't, but it does mean that many others would have found it as difficult as I did. Pamela and I missed the familiarity of the West Side and many of the Jews we were just getting to know. Perhaps if I had not lost my job and Pamela had not suffered a miscarriage, I would have managed in Washington Heights. But my personal difficulties only added to a sense of alienation. Returning to the West Side had a miraculously therapeutic effect.

XLII
DEATH IN THE JEWISH TRADITION

Early in the summer of 1973, I experienced the meaning of Jewish communal *hesed*, kindness. It happened when my mother died.

For a week she lay in a coma at Roosevelt Hospital. Then, on the morning of June 20th, at 3 a.m., we received a call telling us she had passed away. I quickly dressed and hurried to the hospital ward. The medical staff at Roosevelt had done their best to see that my mother had been made as comfortable as possible. Now, as I entered the ward, the on-duty personnel, acting with consideration, allowed me a few minutes alone with her.

I looked down at her and could hardly believe she was really dead. "Blessed be the true Judge," I said in Hebrew. Her jaw was slack, allowing her mouth to hang open. I closed her mouth and recited the *Shema*.

This passage from Deuteronomy (6:4), proclaiming God's unity, is the primary prayer of the Jew; if there is a doubt that it has been said at the hour of death, the first to come to the side of the deceased should say it.

I asked forgiveness for all the heartaches I had ever caused her. Then I covered the body. As the youngest of her four children, I was the last to see, as an infant, her face looking down at me. Now I was the last to see her face in death. No one else in my family would see it again. I remained until the *shomer* (literally, "watchman") arrived. Jewish law requires that the deceased not be left alone until interment is completed. I stayed with her while we awaited the car from the funeral home. All of the obligations to the deceased which I had been physically and emotionally unable to discharge for my father, I now performed for my mother.

At her graveside, I recited the Kaddish, the traditional prayer for the dead, for her. The prayer does not mention death but speaks of the time when God's Messianic kingdom will be established on earth. After the funeral service, my relatives and I filled the grave with earth, following the example of Isaac and Ishmael, who came together to bury their father, Abraham, as is the custom among religious Jews. My sisters "sat *shiva*" with me in my home. During the *shiva*, the initial seven day mourning period, the immediate families of the departed remain at home, receiving the consolation of visitors. They do no work, and all their needs are attended to by others. It was then I learned what being part of a religious community means in time of personal loss. For seven days, my home was filled with people coming to offer me consolation as one "among the other mourners in Zion and Jerusalem," as the traditional liturgical greeting of consolation puts it. Three times a day the *minyan* gathered with me at the time of prayer. And I, as the mourner, was duty-bound to lead the congregation in prayer. It was the first time I had ever been called upon to do so. I was nervous and wondered if I could do it without fumbling. But somehow, with everyone's encouragement, I managed.

Attired in my *tallis,* prayer shawl, and *tefillin,* I gave the call for the congregation of Israel to "Bless *HaShem,* who is to be blessed for ever and ever." Although many years ago at my bar *mitzva,* I had been told, "Now you are a man," I had not, until this moment, grasped the full meaning of Jewish manhood.

On the last day of *shiva,* my teacher, Rabbi Riskin, came to see me. Almost from the very moment of my mother's death, he had given my family assistance that was crucial and indispensable. It was Rabbi Riskin who, after I had awakened him in the early hours of morning, had made all the arrangements with the funeral home; who had made sure that my mother would receive proper burial, even though her death had occurred in the midst of a cemetery workers' strike; who had comforted my family and delivered the heart-rending and poignant eulogy; who had arranged for Cantor Sherwood Goffin to officiate at the grave side; and who ministered to all our needs. (Rabbi Riskin, being a *kohen,* a descendant of Aaron the priest, is forbidden by Jewish law to enter a cemetery.)

I told him that I could not thank him enough for all he had done, and how sorry I was for inconveniencing him. Rabbi Riskin reassured me that I had not done so in any way. Helping the bereaved was part of the obligation he had assumed when he decided to enter the rabbinate. He told me that he usually was involved with several *shivas* every week! The patience and *ahavas yisroel,* love of Israel, of the man are incredible.

XLIII
A HOSTILE ENCOUNTER WITH HEBREW CHRISTIANS

In 1973, the movement known as Jews for Jesus first struck the Jewish community like a bombshell. That same community that had offered "bagels and lox" Judaism to its youth, or no Judaism at all, was now beginning to reap the bitter fruits of apathy, assimilation, and complacency. What did they expect from youths who had everything, and who had tried everything? What did they think was going on when young people began to turn to false gods, Jerry Rubin, Chairman Mao, Timothy Leary, King Drug? Did they consider what would happen when the false gods showed themselves for what they were - false? Could they not foresee that their children might turn from those who had failed them here on earth to intangible, infallible, heaven-dwellers?

Jesus Christ was no longer just a babe in a manger or a figure on a cross. He was a superstar. Every radio blasted it out. Every movie house proclaimed the gospel in stereophonic sound. Jesus was hip! He wore long hair and sandals. Nice Jewish boys and girls, who had never known what made them Jews, began to believe that Jesus could "complete" their Jewishness. These young "completed" Jews were more firmly committed to religion than their parents. The rabbis felt helpless. The parents felt helpless. The Jewish community began to engage in unproductive recriminations.

In 1973, we were living a block south of the building that housed the *Beth Sar Shalom*, and two blocks north of Lincoln Square Synagogue. One thing had changed at *Beth Sar Shalom* since I had been involved with the Hebrew-Christians. The Jews attending services there now were young people who gave each other enthusiastic emotional and religious support.

On occasion, young Jews from *Beth Sar Shalom* would wander over to Lincoln Square Synagogue to talk with us about Jesus; and on occasion some of us, led by two remarkable young rabbis, Ephraim Buchwald and Mordechai Reich, both of whom were knowledgeable in the area of anti-missionary dialectic, would go up there to discuss *Yiddishkeit*, Jewishness, with them.

One Sunday afternoon, my friend, Sam Secofsky, and I went into the *Beth Sar Shalom* just before their services were about to begin. We sat down in the rear and said nothing. But our yarmulkes soon attracted attention, and several people nervously approached us. "We hope you're not from the Jewish Defense League or any other group coming to disturb us," one of them said.

Sam, who was a JDLer, said "We're not here to do anything violent; we're here to observe, and to offer any Jew who is interested in real Judaism, a chance to talk to us.'

Their spokesman, who introduced himself as Reuven, said that we could stay as long as we didn't cause any trouble.

I felt a mixture of emotions as I looked around at the familiar room where I had once been so at home. This same room now represented to me a way of life that was alien and hostile - "the enemy camp."

I recalled having seen Reuven here at the *Beth Sar Shalom* many years ago, but I doubt that he remembered me now nearly twenty years older and fully bearded. At any rate, he gave no sign of recognition. I do not recall seeing any other familiar faces. There were many young people present. One of them approached us and began to witness to us about Jesus, citing "Old Testament" prophecies. When I attempted to answer him by citing several pertinent explanations from the rabbis, he smiled condescendingly and said "Stick to the Bible."

I stopped him almost immediately by asking "Are you Jewish?" He avoided a direct response by making a statement to the effect that "All believers are part of the 'Israel of *God*' (*Galatians 6:16.*)"

"But are you Jewish?," Sam persisted in asking. Again the party-line answer, this time unsmilingly, "God's word tells us: 'He is not a Jew, which is one outwardly; neither is that circumcision, which is outward in the flesh; but he is a Jew, which is one inwardly, and circumcision is that of the heart, in spirit, and not in the letter' (Romans 2:28, 29)," "If you don't mind," I said, "we prefer to speak to Jews, and I find your remarks about circumcision personally insulting, especially coming from someone who presumably is not circumcised, and has not the slightest idea what he is talking about."

Now the full hostility came out. He started shouting, pounding with a fist upon the Bible he was holding in his hand. "Circumcision does not profit. Your fathers who were circumcised were idol worshippers!"

Some of the "brothers" ran up and asked us to please be quiet. I looked at Sam, my face reddening. Knowing what I was feeling, he shook his head. "We're wasting time here," he said. "Obviously we're too Jewish for them. You know, Pharisees," he said with a smile. "Besides, there don't seem to be any Jews here interested in finding out about authentic Judaism."

We came away from the *Beth Sar Shalom* with the following realizations:

Hebrew-Christians do not attempt to proselytize Jews unless they perceive them to be religiously weak and ignorant. Traditional Jews are threatening to them and the attitude toward us is either avoidance or antagonism.

By insisting that we confine ourselves entirely to Biblical texts, they define the nature of the Revelation of Judaism in Christian terms, i.e., denying the validity of the Oral Law. Therefore, in arguing with them, we could always contend that citation of their so called "Messianic prophecies" were invalid arguments since they lacked the proper understanding of Biblical verses that only comes through study of the Oral Law. Furthermore, we could point out the incredible *chutspah,* audacity, in their delimiting our Revelation by saying that it was limited to the written word. To their charge of our incompleteness as Jews, we could point out to the young prospective Hebrew-Christians, the incompleteness of the Christian understanding of the Revelation.

Towards the end of 1974, because of internal problems combined with constant pressure from the Jewish community, the *Beth Sar Shalom* moved from the West 72nd Street location it had occupied for almost thirty years. It was a hollow victory for us. A battle had been won. Nationwide, the war was claiming many Jewish souls.

But there was another side to the coin, the so called *baal tshuvah,* Jews returning to the faith, phenomenon had begun. Many young Jews searching for *HaShem* were finding Him through authentic Judaism. Both in Israel and in the Diaspora, they were turning away from the false gods of the 1960s, and finding their way into newly formed *yeshivot,* religious schools for the *baal tshuvah* before the missionaries could reach them.

Yet, incredibly, some Jewish parents greeted their children's acceptance of *Torah* Judaism the same way other Jewish parents reacted to their children's acceptance of Jesus. In both cases, beneath the parents' stated antagonism to Christianity and to Orthodox Judaism lay the real antagonism - to religion in general. The parents had thrown religion aside as a cumbersome hindrance. They had brought their children up as free thinkers. For them, being religious was a step backwards. Religious observance was only for births, marriages and deaths, and even then it was the rabbi's responsibility to take care of the details. At all other times, it was expendable. As Rabbi Riskin noted, these parents could more easily comprehend their children becoming hippies than they could understand their becoming *hasidim.*"

XLIV
THE AMERICAN JEWISH TRAGEDY

At Lincoln Square Synagogue we were in the midst of the *baal tshuvah* revolution, and it seemed that young Jews were returning to *Torah* in significant numbers. The reality, of course, was that, compared with the total American Jewish community, the number of returning Jews was miniscule. The overwhelming majority of young Jews in the United States continued to drift further away from the mainstream towards assimilation, intermarriage, and apostasy. This was dramatized by attitudes expressed during and immediately after the *Yom Kippur* war.

In the early part of 1974, Rabbi Riskin delivered a depressing sermon one Sabbath. He mentioned a survey, taken just after the *Yom Kippur* war, of Jewish attitudes towards Israel in general, and to the war in particular. It showed that American Jews who exhibited any concern or support for Israel during and after the war tended to be either religious, or if not observant, over forty years old and the children of immigrants. Third and fourth generation Jews from non-religious homes, in their twenties or early thirties were, for the most part, completely unmoved by Israel or her plight. They felt no emotional connection with the Jewish state or the Jewish people.

I decided to check this for myself by asking an acquaintance whose children were in their twenties about their attitudes. She told me that they didn't care about Israel, even during the war when it appeared for a while that Israel might lose. Although this woman, the child of immigrants, was herself concerned about the wellbeing of the Jewish state, she had been unable to pass this involvement on to the next generation in her non-observant home. Being Jewish had no special meaning to her children. Nothing of the chosenness relationship to *HaShem* had been instilled in them. How could they be expected, then, to remain Jewish and to raise children aware of their Jewishness?

As to myself and Pamela, thankfully we were able to raise our child in the traditional Jewish lifestyle.

Before my mother's death, she made me promise to name my first child after my father. Even though my parents' marriage had been less than desirable, yet my mother wished to honor my father's name. She said to me, "He has no one named after him. You must name the first child after him." Although my own relationship with my dad had not been the best, I placed the Jewish obligation that my mother expected from me before my own personal feelings. On March 5, 1975, my daughter Zviah Johannah was born, named for my father, Hershel Zvi, and Pam's grandmother, Johannah.

Rabbi Riskin once told us that when large numbers of Jews were arriving on these shores, seventy-five to one hundred years ago, most of them believed that Judaism simply would not work in the United States. They saw *Torah* commitment as a burden that would prevent them from finding acceptance and earning a living. And they did not expect that their children and grandchildren would take Judaism seriously. Consequently, these immigrants made very few demands on their American-born children, who in turn, made even fewer on their children. By and large, these generations were given much more freedom to behave as they pleased than Jews in Europe had known.

However, without structure, freedom itself can become a terrifying burden. Most human beings do not want to live aimlessly. They need goals in order to find direction. If the Jewish *neshome* is not directed to its *Torah* goal, it may pursue the goals of "the other side," the anti-Semitic radical demagogue, the cult leader, the Nazarene "Messiah," the non-Jewish value system. Not without good cause did our rabbis say: "Do not read *'harut al haluchot'* (engraved upon the tablets); instead read *'herut al haluchot'* (freedom upon the tablets) in commenting on the verse:

> And the tablets were the work of God And the writing was the writing of God, Engraved upon the tablets.
>
> *Exodus 32:16*

The true freedom is the service of *HaShem*.

The Jew has his choice in this world. He can be the servant of *HaShem* or the slave of Pharaoh. Our ancestors had chosen freedom from Pharaoh in order to serve *Hashem*. American Jewish youths, in the closing years of the twentieth Christian century, are again in bondage to a Pharaoh. Some have escaped and found their promised land in the *Torah*. Others believe that they have escaped by joining cult or missionary groups, but in truth they have merely left Pharaoh's realm to wander in the wilderness.

XLV
LINCOLN SQUARE SYNAGOGUE A UNIQUE EXPERIENCE

These are the things of which a person enjoys the fruits in this world, while the capital stands awaiting him in the world to come, namely: honoring father and mother, practice of kindness, timely attendance at the bet midrash morning and evening, graciousness to strangers, visiting the sick, providing for the bride, attending the funeral procession, concentration in prayer, making peace between a man and his fellow; but learning Torah is equal to all of them.

Shabbat 127a

It is axiomatic in Judaism that one cannot remain ignorant and, at the same time, increase one's Jewishness. (See Pirke Avot 1:13, 2:6.) For the Jew, learning occurs on two levels: the practical and the theoretical.

As to the practical, we were fortunate to have developed friendships and associations with Jews well versed in *Torah*. From them we learned the basics of Jewish religious life as it relates to daily observances.

As to more abstract concerns, we benefited from being part of a community in which opportunities to study *Yidishkeit* are very extensive. Lincoln Square Synagogue has, practically, from its inception, maintained a superior evening adult education program offering courses ranging from the fundamentals of Hebrew to advanced Talmud. It allows each student to learn and grow at his or her own pace. Presently, more than a thousand students attend classes weekly. They come from as far away as Long Island, New Jersey and Connecticut. Here they increase their Jewish knowledge in classes led by highly qualified, patient, and empathetic instructors, some of whom are themselves *balei tshuvah*. Pamela and I began attending classes at Lincoln Square shortly after we first came to the synagogue, and what we have gained in terms of understanding Jewish tradition and *HaShem's* ways is incalculable.

In 1974, the synagogue instituted the "beginner's *minyan*," a *shabbat* morning prayer service. Here, under the dynamic and able leadership of Rabbi Ephraim Buchwald, Jews are taught the meaning and structure of Jewish prayer in an atmosphere of joy and *camaraderie*. In 1976, Rabbi Riskin established the unfortunately short lived Lincoln Square Yeshiva, a place of formal learning for young men from non-traditional or limited Jewish religious backgrounds. Many *talmidim*, students, would come evenings, after having put in a full day's work, to study *Torah* together, to daven, pray, and to spend *shabbatot* together. It was at this yeshiva that I first experienced the closeness that can develop within the *chevrusa*, the circle of comrades who learn together, under the guidance of caring and giving teachers. I also formed friendships there that have lasted and remain close.

It is because of such experiences that Lincoln Square Synagogue has become so important to me and my wife. And what is even more appealing in my eyes, is the great effort the synagogue makes to reach out to the Jewish community in general. At Lincoln Square Synagogue, *Torah* study is open to any Jew, regardless of his or her financial means, who sincerely desires to learn. In my opinion, if Judaism is to have a viable future in the United States, it must develop a network of institutions like Lincoln Square Synagogue throughout the country.

XLVI
WHY
I AM AN
OBSERVANT JEW

Gradually I became increasingly involved in anti-missionary activities. During 1974 and 1975, I wrote a series of articles that were published in several Jewish campus newspapers, and I conducted seminars for the now defunct Young Israel Jewish Identity Center. Every Sunday during 1976 and 1977, I taught teenagers how to counter missionary doctrine and methods, at the Morristown Jewish Center in New Jersey. And in 1978, I was in charge of a seminar on Jews and Hebrew-Christians at the Lincoln Square Synagogue Free University. I also began to lecture before Jewish groups about the missionary problem and about my own experiences with Hebrew-Christianity.

Around this time, I started to be invited to speak on radio talk shows. During one program, the host asked what I saw as the basic difference between Christian and Jewish fundamentalism. The interviewer who raised this question could not have sensed how deeply I felt the difference to be. It encompassed a whole range of experiences lasting from the moment of awaking to the very end of the day; from the daily ritual washing of the hands when I first arise, symbolizing the washing away of night-time inactiveness reminiscent of death; to recital of the morning blessings acknowledging my dependence on God and daily acceptance of His commandments; to joining the people of Israel in the community of prayer; to constant praise of God for such basic things as food and clothing, beholding natural phenomena such as the sea, a rainbow, or a storm; to the giving of charity, visiting the sick, comforting the bereaved as required by Jewish law; to studying God's will as interpreted by His teachers, the disciples of the prophets; to sharing with my people their sorrows, joys and hopes; to accepting for myself the Kingship and the Kingdom of Heaven as I lie down to sleep.

I said, in short, that as an observant Jew, my major responsibility is to do *HaShem's* will every day, to be His partner in preparing the way for the coming of the Messiah. I could not abdicate this responsibility by claiming that I was unable to follow His commandments and must, therefore, rely on the death and resurrection of an incarnate god for my salvation. My obligation was to improve this world. I left the other world to *HaShem's* keeping and would rely on His mercy and wisdom to guide me to it when my time came.

In 1978 I became acquainted with Hesh Morgan, executive director of the Anti-Missionary Institute. I learned much from him and I went with him several times to speak to Jews in search of *HaShem*, who had fallen into the missionary net, to bring them back to the ribono-shel-olam, the real Saviour of Israel.

Early in June 1978, Bnai Yeshua, the "Sons of Jesus," hosted the Hebrew-Christian national convention, "Shekina 78," at their headquarters in Stony Brook, New York. On the first day, I drove out there to interview

Jews who had come to accept Jesus as their Messiah. I attended in order to gather material for an article which later appeared in the May 4, 1979 issue of Jewish World, a periodical circulated in Long Island.

Naturally, as an outsider, and especially as an Orthodox Jew, I was treated with suspicion and hostility. Nevertheless, I received enough cooperation from the people I interviewed to enable me to reach several definite conclusions which confirmed ideas I had long held about the fate of Jews who become convinced that the Messiah has already come in the person of Jesus of Nazareth

Thus, I saw that a Jew who believes Jesus to be the Messiah, and who yet wishes to remain a Jew, is completely isolated. He is rejected by other Jews and suspected by gentile Christians. He is separated from the visible Jewish community and given a religious status that tells him he can no longer be accepted "under the law." If he attempts to combine Jewish observances with an expressed belief in Jesus, the gentile Christian church looks upon him as a threat, while the traditional Jewish community feels both insulted and injured. Moreover, after a time, one's Jewishness within a Christian setting becomes less meaningful.

A Jewish woman with two grown sons, both married to gentile Christian woman, became almost hysterical when I questioned the Jewishness of her grand-children. A young man with an eight year involvement in Hebrew-Christianity was obviously embarrassed when speaking about his own marriage to a gentile woman, and he was unable to state with certainty whether or not his own child was Jewish. Even if he had been aware that it is the Jewish mother who passes Jewishness on to her child in the form of the child's Jewish *neshome*, soul, he would have been hard pressed to admit it. It is true that there are verses in Deuteronomy, chapter 7, and elsewhere that have been interpreted by our rabbis that Jewish descent depends upon having a Jewish mother. But Christians probably would not understand these verses as we Jews do. It is a concept of the rabbis, those "blind Pharisees" whose eyes Jesus somehow found neither the time nor the patience to open, who have determined that a Jew is either one with a Jewish mother or one converted to Judaism in accordance with authentic Jewish law. A "Christian" Jew might be proud of being "doubly chosen," but his children and his grandchildren, raised as Protestants, are not likely to feel either the need or the desire to share in that pride.

Christian missionaries use Biblical verses to support their claim that Jesus is the Messiah. Jews who truly understand their heritage, however, cannot accept such an interpretation. In Survival For What?, Zvi Kolitz pointed out that Jews provide living proof that the Messiah has yet to arrive because their redemption is still not at hand. This is evident because, as Maimonides wrote in Laws of Kingship, Israel will return to *Torah* en masse when the Messiah appears. At that time the dispersed of Israel will be gathered and brought to the Holy Land where they will dwell in peace and security, and they will begin to rebuild the sacred Temple in Jerusalem. Moreover, as Maimonides noted, if a man arises and claims to be the Messiah but does not accomplish these things, or is killed, then he is definitely not the Messiah promised to the Jewish people by the ancient prophets. Such is the case with Jesus the Nazarene. Maimonides adds that Jesus cannot be the Messiah because since he appeared, the Jewish people have been subjected by his followers to even greater suffering and persecution.

Despite our historical desire for Messianic peace and security, it should be stressed that Judaism has never been a Messiah-oriented faith. First and foremost, it is *Torah* and *Mitsuah* oriented. If a Jew is engaged in a worthy task and is told, "The Messiah is here," the Talmud admonishes, let him first complete his task and then let him go to see if the Messiah has truly come. The major obligation of Jews is to search for *HaShem*, and to teach their children to do and to hear His commandments which were given at Sinai. Then the path will be made ready for the coming of the real Messiah. But *HaShem* must first find the world truly worthy for this to happen.

XLVII
LOOKING BACKWARD

O Israel, return unto *HaShem* thy God...
Take with you words, and turn to *HaShem*; say unto Him,
Take away all iniquity and receive us graciously;
so we will offer the words of our lips instead of calves.
We will no more say to the work of our hands,
Ye are our gods; for in Thee the fatherless findeth mercy.
I will heal their backsliding, I will love them
freely; for Mine anger is turned away from him.
They that dwell under His shadow shall return.
They shall revive as the corn and grow as the vine.

Hosea 14:2-5, 8

I sat down under His shadow with great delight, and His fruit was sweet to my taste. He brought me to His banqueting house, and His banner over me was love.

Song of Songs 2:3, 4

HaShem hath appeared of old unto me, saying, Yea. I have loved thee with an everlasting love; therefore with *hesed* have I sustained thee.

Jeremiah 31:3

It has been taught; Rabbi Shimon ben Yohai said: Come and see how beloved are Israel in the sight of God, in that to every place to which they were exiled, the Divine Presence went with them.

Talmud, Megillah 29a

When, in retrospect, I consider the events and ideas that have influenced me, I look upon them differently. Experience and maturity have given me another perspective.

It is true that belief in Judaism did not prevent six million Jews during World War II from being sent to their deaths by the "Christian" peoples of Europe. But the Holocaust does not prove that Judaism is a failure. Rather, it points up, in my mind, the inability of 2,000 years of Christian teaching of "love" to penetrate the hearts of many of its followers. One has to wonder whether or not the mission of Christianity is a failure.

It is true that American Jewish religious leaders and teachers during the first half of the twentieth were less than effective in keeping young Jews committed to a Torah way of life, and the Jewish community has paid dearly for this with the loss of millions of its people through assimilation and conversion. But in spite of this, a remnant has remained faithful to the Jewish tradition.

It is true that there are some apparently religious Jews who act in a reprehensible manner, contradictory to the ethical demands of the Torah, thereby desecrating God's Name. And of them the Talmud says: "Woe unto him who studied Torah! Woe unto his teacher who taught him Torah! See how corrupt are his deeds and how ugly his behavior!" (*Yoma* 86a)

It is true that other religious systems of antiquity contained narratives and symbolism similar to our own, the Code of Hammurabi, for example. But they lacked the moral values and influences our sacred works stress.

It is true that there are individual atheists who lead what can be considered moral and ethical lives. But in the main, they have inherited these very moral and ethical values from parents and grandparents who lived within the context of Biblical religion. Unfortunately, our secular society shows very definite signs of abandoning the stabilizing and humanizing attitudes associated with what has been called "the Judeo - Christian heritage."

The world is now reaping the bitter fruit of a society whose guiding philosophy minimizes any spirituality or human concern. In this context, I have come to see an important role for Christianity as a religion which exhorts people to live by the Golden Rule. As Rabbi Hillel originally phrased it, "That which is hateful to thee, do it not to thy brother." Just as Maimonides and other Jewish thinkers concluded that the Christian religion is a valid and worthy path to God for gentiles, I also have come to realize the positive side of Judaism's daughter religion. After all, as the rabbis have taught, there is a place in the world to come for the righteous of all nations.

Certainly, even from an objective point of view, the New Testament, emulating the Hebrew Bible, contains within it much that is inspirational to the believing Christian, especially those verses which speak of the love of God for man and the love of Christians for each other. Yet as far as the Jew is concerned, he must never forget that the same New Testament which contains the comforting message of salvation for Christians, also contains these words:

> I know the blasphemy of them which say they are Jews, and are not, but are the synagogue of Satan.
>
> *Revelation 2:9*

> Behold, I will make them of the synagogue of Satan, which say they are Jews, and are not, but do lie; Behold, I will make them to come and worship (Jesus).
>
> *Revelation 3:9*

> … the Jews who both killed the lord Jesus, and their own prophets, and have persecuted us; and they please not God, and are contrary to all men.
>
> *First Thessalonians 2:14, 15*

Then said Jesus to those Jews which believed in him. I know that ye are Abraham's seed; but ye seek to kill me because my word hath no place in you. If God were your father, ye would love me. Ye are of your father the devil, and the lusts of your father ye will do. He that is of God heareth God's words; ye therefore hear them not because ye are not of God.

John 8:31, 37,42,44,47

The ultimate problem confronting Jews, *vis-a-vis* Christians, is the insistence, by the missionizing segment of Christianity's adherents, that links its very being to the ultimate conversion of all Jews. As long as attempts at proselytization continue, Jews must remain wary of the positive aspects of Christianity.

In examining religious life in the United States, we must accept the importance of religious pluralism and tolerance but, at the same time, protect religiously ignorant Jews from the influence of missionaries. The Jewish community has not been particularly successful to date because it has been more concerned with fighting for religious freedom and equality. Had the Jewish leadership and the community been more willing to extend their concern to countless others like me, there would now be many more Jews within the ranks of the committed.

As I think back on my encounter with the Christian missionaries, my saddest thought is that they were the first to tell me that there is a God in heaven who loves me. Yet this is the essential message of the Torah. God cared so much for the Jewish people that He acted to remove them from Egyptian slavery. He then brought the Jews to the foot of Mt. Sinai, and there gave them His holy laws by which to know Him, and by which to live. All this shows me that God cares about, and loves, the Jewish people. But talk about God's love is embarrassing for modern man in general, and for many contemporary Jews in particular. Whenever I speak before Jewish audiences about the importance of informing young, non-involved Jews that "there is a God in heaven who loves," I am usually told, - as a conservative rabbi who hosted a radio show on which I appeared once said to me, "That sounds Christian." Jews have even stated to me that "Judaism holds no such doctrine." But one has only to look into the Torah to see how untrue this is.

God has revealed His love for Israel many times over. For most people, however, God's love reaches them through their fellow human beings. In my opinion, for Jews this takes the form of ahavas Yisroel, the concern Jews have for their fellow Jews. We read in our prayer book, for instance, each Sabbath immediately preceding the appearance of a new moon, "Gather our dispersed people from the four corners of the earth because all Israel are brothers." (The word I have translated as "brothers," haverim, carries the root meaning of "people who are tightly bound together.") And further, in the Talmud (Shevuot 39a), we are told, "All Israel is responsible each one for the other." In the written Torah itself we find:

Thou shall not hate thy brother in thy heart; thou shalt surely rebuke thy neighbor, and not bear sin upon him. Thou shalt love thy neighbor as thyself. I am *HaShem.*

Leviticus 19:17, 18

From this we learn that allowing any religiously ignorant Jew to continue in his ignorance is to bear the sin that he commits in his ignorance, and the greatest sin we bear is that, by neglecting to tell him, "I am *HaShem*", we do not show that we love him as we love ourselves.

Perhaps the most poignant teaching regarding Jewish responsibility and commitment to fellow Jews is based upon the following verses:

> These are the generations of Noah; Noah was a just man and perfect in his generation, and Noah walked with God.
>
> *Genesis 6:9*

> Thus did Noah; according to all that God commanded him, so did he.
>
> *Genesis 6:22*

The Rabbis asked why Noah, who was just and perfect, and acted "according to all that *HaShem* commanded him," was not chosen, rather than Abraham, to be the father of the Jewish people. They answered that while Noah was "perfect in his generation", he would not have been considered so, had he lived in the generation of Abraham. Noah "walked with God." but not with people. Therefore, although Noah did all that God commanded, he did not make any additional effort to bring his fellow human beings back to God so that they might avoid destruction.

In contrast, the rabbis note that Abraham, our father, "got souls" (Genesis 12:5), i.e., he cared enough to go out and teach people. Abraham, our father, walked "in front of God" and would be considered "perfect" not only in his generation, but, without qualification, at any time (Genesis 17:1). When Noah learned of God's plan to destroy the world, he went into his ark without alerting his fellow human beings. But when Abraham was told of God's plan to destroy Sodom and Gomorrah, he pleaded with Him to spare those cities (Genesis 18:20). For such compassion, Abraham well deserves the appellation, "Father of the Jewish People." What he was willing to do for non-Jews, should we not at least be willing to do for our Jewish brethren?

In the 1970s, many in the United States experienced a religious awakening. Jews and gentiles alike who, tired of materialism, and frustrated by a growing inability to deal effectively with crime, immorality, loss of values, and untrustworthiness in human institutions and their leadership, began to change their lifestyles. For disenfranchised Jews, living in uncaring, status-seeking Jewish communities, the attempt in many cases was particularly difficult and painful. It need not have been, nor must it be. According to Rabbi Riskin, this is the last generation of lost, young Jews who can be won back to Torah in relatively large numbers before assimilation and the missionaries claim them. Dare we shirk this task? We ought not if we want to follow what our sages have taught- "He who saves one soul, it is as though he saved the world."

The synagogue could play a vital role in reaching out to meet the challenge of Jews seeking *HaShem*. One might say that synagogues have an obligation, a mission, to errant sons and daughters. But this mission has not been realized. Regrettably, there is still too much concern with image, with who does or does not "look right."

Most synagogues in the United States - Reform, Conservative, and Orthodox have failed. Synagogues, more often than not, have become predominantly social clubs for the middle class, and this has resulted in turning off countless numbers of Jews who could have been otherwise helped in discovering *HaShem*. Thankfully, some Jews still exist who are able to discover Him in spite of synagogues.

Our latent source for a resurgence of Jewish religious life lies within the family. The home, in fact, has traditionally been the main religious influence on each generation. It is family that inculcates in children their sense of Jewishness. The home is Judaism's crucible. It is here that the teachings of the Jewish day schools are put into practice through daily activities, the Sabbath and holiday observance.

The Jewish adult is shaped more by memories of childhood events in the home than by those in the synagogue. And it is experiences involving one's family that remain most vivid - memories of helping one's mother bake Sabbath loaves, of watching her light Sabbath and festival candles, of tasting kiddush wine from a metal cup, of singing songs round a table with family and friends, of smelling spices as the Sabbath departs, of sitting in a succah, the makeshift dwelling place used during the holiday of Succoth, of feeling one's father's warm hands on one's head as he recited the traditional parental blessing, and of hearing praise after reciting the Passover Four Questions for the first time. These are the sort of memories that nourish and sustain Jewish children as they grow up and take on religious commitments for reasons other than parental insistence. Thus is tradition passed from one generation to the next. It has been so for thousands of years.

In our unfortunate generation, however, family guidance has been so greatly weakened it has become obligatory for the Jewish community to extend its concern beyond its own particular children to all searching and uncommitted Jews. We must continuously keep in mind that *"Kawl yisrael aravim zeh el zeh,"* - All Israel is responsible for one another.

XLVIII
LOOKING FORWARD

The subtitle of this book is, One Man's Search for a Meaningful Faith. In a sense, with my return to the Jewish people and to my God as an observant Jew, my odyssey is at an end. However, in another sense, the quest for *HaShem* is never over. A Jew must strive to come closer and closer to Him for as long as he lives. By one's deeds and through study of His word, every Jew must attempt to bring the *tamid*, the perpetual daily sacrifice, before His altar. We must continually seek to deepen our commitment to Him and to our fellow Jews who are created in His image.

The souls of my parents have "gone on to their world," in the words of the *Yizkor* memorial prayer:

> They are bound up in the bond of life along with the souls of Abraham, Isaac, Jacob, Sarah, Rebecca, Rachel and Leah, and with all the other righteous ones in Gan Eden, paradise. The compassionate God who dwells in the heights, may He grant them perfect rest under the wings of His Shechinah, Divine Spirit, in the realm of the holy and pure ones who shine like the resplendent firmament. May *HaShem* be their heritage, and may they rest in His peace. Amen.

My father died before he could see my return to Judaism, and the many difficulties that resulted in the estrangement between us remained unresolved to my regret. Perhaps, had he still been living when I became Orthodox, I might have found the strength to reach out and draw us closer to one another. As it was, I never even sat *shiva* for him. King Solomon spoke truly when he said:

> That which is crooked cannot be made straight and that which is lacking cannot be numbered.
>
> *Ecclesiastes 1:15*

My mother passed away before she could witness the birth of my daughter. Although she was never reconciled with my father, I honored one of her final requests. *Shloymeleh*," she said to me, while that debilitating illness was taking her away from us, "Your father has no one named after him. Promise that you will name your first child after him."

While my parents separated from each other in life, they return to me each year, united in the flames of the two *yortsayt* glasses I light in their memory. At the holidays when all of committed Israel comes together in joy and love, I reach out to them through the *Yizkor* prayers. I recite the *Kaddish* on the anniversaries of their passing. And I see them reflected in the eyes of my daughter who bears a feminized form of my father's name, as my mother requested. Moreover, because my parents and their forefathers refused to worship other gods, when the alternative was exile or even death, I felt the obligation to raise my daughter in the Jewish tradition. And today she is a loving child to me, fully within the committed worldwide congregation of Israel and she has passed on our religious heritage to my grand daughter, Charlize Elsa, named after my mother CHARNA and Pam's mother Elsa.

I am my child's past in an unbroken line reaching back to Abraham, our father, and Sarah, our mother, whom *HaShem* took out of Chaldean Ur and separated for Himself, to found a special people. And she is our future, the next link in an unbroken chain that will extend to the days of the Messiah - the TRUE Messiah. On the first two nights of Passover and at the departure of the Sabbath each week, we pray that HaShem will hasten the coming of Messiah. May *HaShem*, grant that we be the Messiah's coheralds along with Eliyahu Hanavi, Elijah the prophet, by doing His commandments, as was uttered by His prophet:

> Remember ye the Torah of Moses My servant
> Which I commanded unto him in Horeb,
> For all Israel, with decrees and laws.
> Behold, I will send you Elijah the prophet
> Before the coming of the great and awesome day of *HaShem*
> And he shall turn the heart of the fathers to the children
> And the heart of the children to their fathers.
> Lest I should come and strike the earth with destruction.
> Behold, I will send you Elijah the prophet
> Before the coming of the great and awesome day of *HaShem*
> And he shall turn the heart of the fathers to the children
> *Malachi (4:4-6)*

XLIX
AFTERWORD

There is no doubt that Lincoln Square Synagogue and its rabbis played a pivotal role in my life, both by helping me become aware of my Jewish heritage and by strengthening my religious commitment. However, I want to stress that no one institution or religious personality can bear the total burden of a "mission to the Jews." It is important to realize that most Jews do not associate regularly with rabbis and scholars. Jews live with others like themselves - with Jews concerned with everyday matters in whose company they study, pray and hopefully, receive the support necessary for spiritual growth.

Religious institutions can provide a proper atmosphere for meaningful Jewish experiences, and rabbis can provide *halachic,* religious, decisions. But individual Jews must ultimately draw strength from fellow Jews to supplement the God-given strength they find within themselves.

For those readers who would like to learn more about the Jewish heritage, a bibliography follows that covers many important aspects of Judaism, and also an appendix listing religious groups that will extend formal hospitality, as well as offer opportunities for study, and to become active in the religious Jewish community. May the number increase. Amen.

BIBLIOGRAPHY
A. On Jews and Judaism.

AGNON, Y.S.: Days of Awe, Schocken, New York.

ARTZ, MAX: Justice & Mercy, Holt, Rinehart & Winston, New York.

BEN ISAIAH, ABRAHAM & SHARFMAN, BENJAMIN: The Pentateuch & Rashi's Commentary (A Linear Translation into English), S.S. & R. Publishing, Brooklyn.

BERKOVITZ, ELIEZER: Faith After The Holocaust, KTAV, New York.

BIRNBAUM, PHILIP: Daily Prayer Book, Hebrew Publishing Company, New York.

CARMEL, ABRAHAM: So Strange My Path, Bloch, New York.

CASPER, BERNARD M.: An Introduction To Jewish Bible Commentary, Thomas Yoseloff, New York.

COHEN REV. DR. A.: The Soncino Chumash (The Five Books of Moses), Soncino, London.

COHN, JACOB: The Royal Table (An Outline of the Dietary Laws of Israel), Feldheim, New York.

DAVIS, AVRAHAM: The Metsudah *Siddur*: Daily Prayers, Metsudah Publications/Zion Tallis Book, New York

DE SOLA POOL, DAVID: The Traditional Prayer Book for Sabbath & Festivals, Behrman House, New York.

DONIN, HAYIM HALEVY: To Be a Jew (A Guide to Jewish Observance in Contemporary Life). Basic Books, New York.

FACKENHEIM, EMIL L.: God's Presence in History, Harper Torchbooks, New York.

GOLDIN, HYMAN E. A Treasury of Jewish Holidays, Twayne, New York.

GOODMAN, PHILIP: Passover Anthology, Jewish Publication Society, Philadelphia. Purim Anthology, Jewish Publication Society, Philadelphia. Rosh HaShanah Anthology, Jewish Publication Society, Philadelphia. Shavuot Anthology, Jewish Publication Society, Philadelphia. Sukkot & Simhat *Torah* Anthology, Jewish Publication Society, Philadelphia. *Yom Kippur* Anthology, Jewish Publication Society, Philadelphia

GRAYZEL, SOLOMON: A History of the Jews, Jewish Publication Society, Philadelphia.

GRUNFELD, I.: The Sabbath (A Guide to its Understanding & Observance), Feldheim, New York.

HESCHEL, ABRAHAM JOSHUA: The Earth is the Lord's, Harper Torchbooks, New York. The Sabbath, Harper Torchbooks, New York.

JACOBS, LOUIS: Faith,, Basic Books, New York.

JACOBSON, B.S.: Days of Awe, Sinai Publications, Tel Aviv. Meditations on the *Siddur*, Sinai Publications, Tel Aviv. Meditations on the *Torah*, Sinai Publica tions, Tel Aviv. The Weekday *Siddur*, Sinai Publications, Tel Aviv.

JUNGREIS, ESTHER: The Jewish Soul on Fire, Morrow, New York.

KAPLAN, ARYEH: Love Means Reaching Out, National Conference on Synagogue Youth, New York.

KOLITZ, ZVI: Survival For What?, Philosophical Library, New York.

MILLER, AVIGDOR: Behold A People, Balshon, Brooklyn. *Torah* Nation, Balshon, Brooklyn.

MILLGRAM, ABRAHAM: Jewish Worship, Jewish Publication Society, Philadelphia.

MUNK, ELIE: The World of Prayer, Feldheim, New York.

OPPENHEIM, MICHA FALK: The Study and Practice of Judaism: A Selected, Annotated List, *Torah* Resources, 951 56th Street, Brooklyn.

PRAGER, DENNIS & TELUSHKIN, JOSEPH: Eight Questions People Ask About Judaism., Tze Ulmad, Whitestone, New York.

SCHAUSS, HAYYIM: Guide to Jewish Holy Days, Schocken, New York.

SCHILLER, MAYER: The Road Back, Feldheim, New York.

SOLIS-COHEN, EMILY: Hanukkah, Jewish Publication Society, Philadelphia.

STEINBERG, MILTON: The Making of the Modern Jew, Behrman House, New York.

WAGSCHAL, S.: A Practical Guide to Kashruth (The Dietary Laws), Gateshead Foundation for *Torah*, Gateshead, England.

WOUK, HERMAN: This is my God (The Jewish Way of Life), Pocket Books, New York.

B. On Judaism's Answer to Missionary Christianity.

ANONYMOUS: The Disputation, Scholarly Publications, Salford, England.

BAECK, LEO: Judaism & Christianity, Atheneum, New York.

BERGER, DAVID & WYSCHOGROD, MICHAEL: Jews & Jewish Christianity, KTAV, New York

DANNIEL BENJAMIN: Jesus, Jews & Gentiles, Arco, New York.

DRIVER, SAMUEL R. & NEUBERGER, ADOLF: The "Suffering Servant" of Isaiah According to the Jewish Interpreters, Hermon Press, New York.

JUNGREIS, ESTHER: Everything You Always Wanted to Know About Jesus, But Were Afraid to Ask, Hineini, North Woodmere, New York.

KAPLAN, ARYEH: The Real Messiah, National Conference of Synagogue Youth, New York.

LEVINE, SAMUEL: You Take Jesus, I'll Take God, Hamorah Press, Los Angeles.

SARACHEK, JOSEPH: The Doctrine of the Messiah in Medieval Jewish Literature, Hermon Press, New York.

SCHOEPS, HANS JOACHIM: The Jewish-Christian Argument, Holt, Rinehart & Winston, New York.

SIGEL, GERALD: The Jew and the Christian Missionary: A Jewish Response to Missionary Christianity, Ktav, New York.

SILVER, ABBA HILLEL: Where Judaism Differed, Macmillan, New York.

TROKI, ISAAC: Faith Strengthened, Hermon Press, New York.

WEISS-ROSMARIN, TRUDE: Judaism & Christianity, Jonathan David, New York.

SOME GROUPS OFFERING HOSPITALITY
AND HELP TO THOSE WISHING TO EXPERIENCE
AND LEARN ABOUT *TORAH* JUDAISM

Rabbi Kasriel Kastel" *Chabad*-Lubavitch 770 Eastern Parkway Brooklyn, NY 11213 (212) 778-4270*

Lincoln Square Synagogue 200 Amsterdam Avenue New York, NY 10023 (212) 874-6100

National Conference of Synagogue Youth 116 East 27th Street New York, NY 10016 (212) 725-3420

Hineini 440 Hungry Harbor Road North Woodmere, NY 11581 (516) 791-1231

Drisha (women's group c/o West Side Institutional Synagogue 122 West 76th Street New York, NY 10023 (212) 595-0307

New England Chassidic Center - Bostoner Rebbe, Levi Horow 1710 Beacon Street, Brookline, MA 02146 (617) 734-5100

Shor Yoshuv Institute 1526 Central Avenue Far Rockaway, NY 11691 (212) 327-2048

Rabbi Shlomo Carlebach 888 Seventh Avenue New York, NY 10019 (212) 265-4300

Chizuk Agudah 5 Beekman Street New York, NY 10038 (212) 791-1800

Agudah Hotline to Judaism (24 Hour) (212) 791-1848

Hebrew Institute of Riverdale 3700 Henry Hudson Parkway, Bronx, NY 10463 (212) 796-4730

Jews For Judaism
P.O. Box 24903
Los Angeles, CA 90024 (213)557-2566

Jews For Judaism
P.O. Box 15059
Baltimore, MD 21208 (301)764-7788

Havurat Yisrael
106-20 70th Avenue
Forrest Hills, NY 11367 (718)261-5500

Yeshiva Of The West Side
Cong. Kehilath Jacob
305 West 79th Street
New York, NY 10024 (212)580-2391

Chabad has locations throughout the United States and Canada Rabbi Kastel will supply the address and phone number of the most accessible *Chabad* house or affiliate.

THE FOLLOWING IS FROM THE ORIGINAL COVER BIO.

Isaac Mozeson writes:
Book Review Editor, Judaica Book News

In *From Jesus To Judaism,* Shlomoh Sherman wends his way home despite the unconcern of the Jewish community. This brave, brutally frank autobiography indicts the apathetic Jewish soul stiflers as much as the Evangelical soul-snatchers.

His several year flirtation with Hebrew-Christianity was the only spiritual fulfillment his disinterested East Bronx family would allow him. The shining, singing faces at the messianic *Beth Sar Shalom* contrasted sharply with indifference at home and inhospitality at synagogues of all de nominations. If anything, young Shlomoh escaped to Jesus.

It was the early 1950's. Six million Jews lay murdered in still-fresh graves. Millions of American Jewish youth would be buried by the push away generation that held sway fifteen years before outreach and *baal-tshuvah* movements would surface.

"You are not dressed properly and your head is not covered. You don't look right. Please leave." I was shocked! No one stood up for me. It was as though my own brother had stuck a knife in me. I yelled out, "You son of a bitch! On the day you die maybe you won't look right to God!" I turned my back and stormed out.

That day was *Yom Kippur* of 1955. I was not to step back into a synagogue for over ten years.

Jacket design: Sally Billig
Decalogue Books 7 North MacQuesten Parkway Mount Vernon, NY 10550 Printed in USA 9/83
ISBN 0-915474-03-4

Photo Big Joe Kaplan

At first glance, Shlomoh Sherman's autobiography might appear to be depicting the life of any number of his contemporaries. He was raised in a deteriorating, lower-middle class, Yiddish-speaking Jewish neighborhood in the Bronx, educated at public institutions (BA in Spanish from City College of New York, MA in Linguistics from Hunter, and AAS in Data Processing from Manhattan Community College), and inducted into the U.S. Army in which he served for two years in Germany. Aside from these experiences which were shared with many others of his generation, the similarities are few.

Mr. Sherman, Jewish by birth, accepted Jesus of Nazareth as the Jewish Messiah while still in his teens. He joined a proselytizing group, known as Hebrew-Christians that took a personal interest in him unlike any he had ever known within the Jewish community. He remained with the Hebrew-Christians for two years, and then. Mr. Sherman severed all ties with Christianity. His subsequent search for a more meaningful religious association, lasting over a decade eventually led him to encounters with traditional Jewish groups who understood the importance of reaching out to unaffiliated Jews especially those seeking a strong commitment to an authentic Jewish life style and an intense involvement within the Community of Israel

Shlomoh Sherman explains how Christian missionaries were once able to lead him to a belief in Jesus, why he became disillusioned with Christianity, and what impelled him to examine and ultimately to embrace Orthodox Judaism. From Jesus to Judaism presents a totally Jewish option to any Jew who has ever been enticed by such groups as Jews for Jesus and the cults.

Appendices
Jews And Jesus

IS JESUS THE MESSIAH?

This question, answered in the affirmative by many Christians, is pertinent only to Jews.

When Christians witness to gentiles, to convince them to accept Jesus as their deity, they will present him as Savior, Son of God, and God Himself.

The one thing that they don't do is to present him to the nonJew as the Messiah. To the average gentile, "Messiah" is devoid of any real emotional meaning since the very messianic concept is only meaningful to Jews who came up with the idea of a Super Rescuer.

However, when Christian missionaries approach Jews in order to bring them to Christ, the first thing they will say is that Jesus is "your Messiah". His other designations such as savior or God are left for a later time if the witnessing is successful. Initially, Jews might be uncomfortable with accepting a man as God.

Many ethnic groups have an idea of a coming Superman who will restore them to their former glory and will alter the world, in fact, the universe, to a place of Paradise, that is, some form of Lost Eden.

But "the Messiah", that is, an individual especially Anointed by Heaven to be, not only King of the Jews but King of the Cosmos, with planet Earth as it's center and with its capital, the City on a Hill, Jerusalem. In fact, the very Hebrew word MESHIACH means "anointed" as does the Greek XRISTOS which Christianity appropriated from Jews.

But does Jesus really qualify to be Israel's Messiah? A look at the New Testament will give us an answer.

The witnessing approach to Jews may begin with two questions, namely:

"Did you know that Jesus was a Jew?"

"If you Jews don't consider Jesus to be the Messiah, do you, at least, think he is a prophet or a great rabbi?"

Here is a conversation I would have with the person asking the first question.

I. You ask me if I know that Jesus was a Jew.
He. Yes.
I. Do you believe in Jesus as your savior?
He. Yes I do.
I. Do you believe that he is alive somewhere?
He. Of course.
I. Yet you used the past tense. You said he WAS a Jew. So do you not think he is Jewish any longer?

He may be at a loss as to how to answer but Christians whom I have asked about Jesus' Jewishness, say he is not Jewish now. Let's see what Christian Scripture has to say about it.

> Wherefore henceforth know we no man after the flesh: yea, though we have known Christ after the flesh, yet now henceforth know we him no more.
>
> *Second Corinthians: Chapter 5:16*

Paul, the creator of Christianity, makes it clear here that Jesus is no longer the Jewish man he once was. How can he be? He is now a deity; a god has no ethnic identity. Ethnicity is reserved for people. That being the case, how can the fact of Jesus Christ's so-called Jewishness [when he walked the earth] be significant to me? The Jewish Messiah will be born Jewish and will remain Jewish even after his death. +

Here is a conversation I would have with the person asking the second question.

If Jews don't consider Jesus to be the messiah, then whatever else he may have been is beside the point. Either he is the Messiah or not. And Jews don't consider Jesus to have been anything. In fact, Jews don't think much about Jesus. He has no place in our lives. We do worse than reject him. We ignore him. Let's see what Christian Scripture has to say about it.

The question is not new. In fact, it goes all the way back to the time that Christianity began. It goes back to the Gospel according to Matthew.

> When Jesus came into the coasts of Caesarea Philippi, he asked his disciples, saying, Whom do men say that I the Son of man am? And they said: Some say that thou art John the Baptist: some, Elias; and others, Jeremias, or one of the prophets. He saith unto them, But whom say ye that I am? And Simon Peter answered and said, Thou art the Christ, the Son of the living God. And Jesus answered and said unto him, Blessed art thou, Simon Barjona: for flesh and blood hath not revealed it unto thee, but my Father which is in heaven. And I say also unto thee, That thou art Peter, and upon this rock I will build my church; and the gates of hell shall not prevail against it. And I will give unto thee the keys of the kingdom of heaven: and whatsoever thou shalt bind on earth shall be bound in heaven: and whatsoever thou shalt loose on earth shall be loosed in heaven. Then charged he his disciples that they should tell no man that he was Jesus the Christ. From that time forth began Jesus to shew unto his disciples, how that he must go unto Jerusalem, and suffer many things of the elders and chief priests and scribes, and be killed, and be raised again the third day. Then Peter took him, and began to rebuke him, saying, Be it far from thee, Lord: this shall not be unto thee. But he turned, and said unto Peter, Get thee behind me, Satan: thou art an offense unto me: for thou savourest not the things that be of God, but those that be of men.
>
> *Matthew 16:13-23*

Jesus tells Peter that no person has said that Jesus is the Messiah; Peter has gotten a message direct from Heaven. This tells us that Jesus himself has not told anyone that he is the Messiah. Furthermore, he admonishes his followers not to tell anyone that he is the Messiah. What can he be hiding from? Does he mean that once he does make that known, he will be tested and harassed by the authorities, especially the Romans? Does he mean he will reveal his messiahship when he is ready to be killed, and not before?

Aside from the fact that Peter addresses Jesus as the son of God [a Christological idea], he looks upon him as the Jewish Messiah, meaning that the Messiah cannot be overcome by his enemies or suffer death at their hands. The Jewish Messiah overcomes all obstacles to his reestablishing the Kingdom of Israel which means establishing the Kingdom of Heaven on earth. Not only will the Messiah succeed in his mission, but the most important thing about his mission will be the disappearance of antisemitism. Peter does not want to hear that the messiah, Jesus, will be actually killed. So he contradicts Jesus' death wish. How does Jesus respond? He calls Peter SATAN! This is the disciple whom he has just called the Rock of his Church, his lieutenant. And yet, in the next breath, Peter is Satan. And why not? What is Satanic about being the real Jewish Messiah according to Christianity? Let's see. To quote Christian missionaries, Search the Scripture.

The beginning of the gospel of Jesus Christ, the Son of God; John did baptize in the wilderness and preach the baptism of repentance for the remission of sins. And there went out unto him all the land of Judaea, and they of Jerusalem, and were all baptized of him in the river of Jordan, confessing their sins. And John was clothed with camel's hair, and with a girdle of a skin about his loins, and he did eat locusts and wild honey; And preached, saying, there cometh one mightier than I after me, the latchet of whose shoes I am not worthy to stoop down and unloose. I indeed have baptized you with water: but he shall baptize you with the Holy Ghost. And it came to pass in those days, that Jesus came from Nazareth of Galilee, and was baptized of John in Jordan. And straightway coming up out of the water, he saw the heavens opened, and the Spirit like a dove descending upon him: And there came a voice from heaven, saying, Thou art my beloved Son, in whom I am well pleased. And immediately the spirit driveth him into the wilderness. And he was there in the wilderness forty days, tempted of Satan.

Mark 1:1-13

Then was Jesus led up of the Spirit into the wilderness to be tempted of the devil. And when he had fasted forty days and forty nights, he was afterward an hungered. And when the tempter came to him, he said, If thou be the Son of God, command that these stones be made bread. But he answered and said, It is written, Man shall not live by bread alone, but by every word that proceedeth out of the mouth of God. Then the devil taketh him up into the holy city, and setteth him on a pinnacle of the temple, and saith unto him, If thou be the Son of God, cast thyself down: for it is written, He shall give his angels charge concerning thee: and in their hands, they shall bear thee up, lest at any time thou dash thy foot against a stone. Jesus said unto him, It is written again, Thou shalt not tempt the Lord thy God. Again, the devil taketh him up into an exceeding high mountain, and sheweth him all the kingdoms of the world, and the glory of them; And saith unto him, All these things will I give thee, if thou wilt fall down and worship me. Then saith Jesus unto him, Get thee hence, Satan: for it is written, Thou shalt worship the Lord thy God, and him only shalt thou serve. Then the devil leaveth him, and, behold, angels came and ministered unto him.

Matthew 4:1-11

Mark is the earliest written New Testament gospel. Mark's account of Jesus' story starts with his baptism. It is at his baptism that he becomes the son of God. That is, he is an ordinary human being who becomes divine by God's adoption. Mark has no story of Jesus's miraculous birth from a virgin. When Mark wrote, about 70CE, Christology had not yet advanced to make Jesus God. Immediately after he becomes Christ, Mark tells us that he went into the wilderness to be tempted by Satan. However, the details of what has become known as the story of the Temptation of Christ are left for Matthew, the second written gospel.

Think about why this story of Jesus' temptation comes at the very beginning of his mission as Christ. Let's look at the details of the Temptation.

The first thing the devil asks him to do is to turn stones into bread. Jews believe that the Messiah will rid the world of hunger, and also of poverty, sickness and want. But Jesus refuses this request.

Secondly, the devil asks him to put himself in mortal danger, relying on Heaven to rescue him. Jews believe that the Messiah is invulnerable to any kind of harm. Jesus also refuses this request to put himself in harm's way. In fact, at the end of his earthly mission, he will offer himself up to the Romans to be executed as a rebel.

Thirdly, the devil offers him dominion over all the nations in the world. Not only does he also refuse this request but he tells Satan to get out of his sight, similar to what he told Peter.

This story tells the reader right from the start that Jesus is NOT the Messiah that the Jews expect. He is something other. It tells the reader that the Messiah that the Jews expect is Satanic. Jesus lets Peter know that he is looking for the "things of men", a warrior whose kingdom is of this world, not "the things that be of God", a savior whose kingdom is not here on earth. [John 18:36 Jesus answered (Pontius Pilate), "My kingdom is not of this world."]

The New Testament book, Acts of the Apostles, tells what happened with Jesus' disciples after his crucifixion and resurrection. Here are some verses from its opening chapter.

The resurrected Jesus shows himself to his disciples.

> And, behold, two of them went that same day to a village called Emmaus, which was from Jerusalem about threescore furlongs. And it came to pass, that, while they communed together and reasoned, Jesus himself drew near, and went with them. And he said unto them. What manner of communications are these that ye have one to another, as ye walk, and are sad? And the one of them, whose name was Cleopas, answering said unto him, Art thou only a stranger in Jerusalem, and hast not known the things which are come to pass there in these days? And he said unto them, What things? And they said unto him, Concerning Jesus of Nazareth, which was a prophet mighty in deed and word before God and all the people: And how the chief priests and our rulers delivered him to be condemned to death, and have crucified him. But we trusted that it had been he which should have redeemed Israel: and beside all this, today is the third day since these things were done.
>
> *Luke 24: 13-21*

They say that he is just a "mighty prophet" but they also believe he may have been the Messiah. And they are sad because he died rather than bringing the Kingdom of Heaven. They declare what Jews declare; that the Messiah is a special prophet, NOT some aspect of the divine.

> When they, therefore, were come together, they asked of him, saying, Lord, wilt thou at this time restore again the kingdom to Israel? And he said unto them, It is not for you to know the times or the seasons, which the Father hath put in his own power.
>
> *Acts 1:6-7*

In other words, NO! You're still expecting me to be the Messiah the Jews want. I'm not he. I'm not bringing any Kingdom of Heaven or Messianic Age here. That's not who I am.

The religion of Christ was adopted as the official faith of the Roman Empire. That religion evolved to become the Roman Catholic Church and the Holy Roman Empire. Even with the rise of the Protestant heresy, only the outer trappings of Catholicism were ejected. The basic Roman theology of the New Testament was retained. Christ became a Roman god who cannot be Israel's Messiah.

So again, "Do you Jews consider Jesus to be your Messiah?" has to be answered with an emphatic NO!

+ Although a friend made the statement that when Jesus returns to earth, he will return in bodily form, and he will be circumcised. So perhaps he'll rejoin the Jewish People at that time!

CHRISTIANITY'S MISSION TO THE JEWS

This is a story told to me by my rabbi, Shlomo Riskin. In the mid1950s, Israeli Prime Minister David Ben-Gurion was interviewed by an American reporter who asked him the following question:

> "Mr. Prime Minister, when President Eisenhower opens a meeting of his cabinet, he begins with a prayer. Why don't you open the session of the KENESET with a prayer?"

Supposedly, Ben-Gurion gave the reporter this response:

> "You have to understand that President Eisenhower, as a Christian, has one major religious responsibility [*MITSVAH*], and that is to acknowledge Jesus as his savior and to tell other people about that belief. I, on the other hand, have 613 religious responsibilities, and I have difficulty in performing even a few."

When Jews ask why some Christians are so eager to convert nonChristians to their faith, they show their ignorance of Christianity's Great Commission. This is understandable. Due to past persecutions, Jews tend to shy away from anything having to do with Christianity, including its scriptures.

What is the Great Commission?

According to the New Testament, after his Resurrection, Jesus gave his disciples this command:

> Therefore go and make disciples of all nations, baptizing them in the name of the Father and of the Son and of the Holy Spirit, and teaching them to obey everything I have commanded you. And surely I am with you always, to the very end of the age.
>
> *Matthew 28:19-20*

The disciples, obeying their savior's commission to advance the salvation of all mankind, made this declaration:

> For this is what the Lord has commanded us: 'I have made you a light for the Gentiles, that you may bring salvation to the ends of the earth.
>
> *Acts 13:47*

Evangelizing Christians who are seriously dedicated to this Commission feel that they have no alternative but to carry out the One Great Commandment of their Master. They are IMPELLED to do this one important Christian *MITSVAH*.

But it is even more than this. In the Gospel According to Luke, Jesus tells his disciples a parable about a certain man who makes a supper party and sends his servants out into the streets to invite people to come in for the feast. And for those who will not accept the invitation, then:

> And the lord said unto the servant[s], Go out into the highways and hedges, and COMPEL THEM to come in, that my house may be filled. (emphasis mine)
>
> *Luke 14:23*

Not only are Christ's followers to persuade all people to join his covenant. They are to persuade by COMPULSION. Is it any wonder then, based on these scriptural admonitions, that history is filled with Crusades and Inquisitions, and even pogroms?

In the modern era, Crusades, Inquisitions, and pogroms are prohibited by law, at least in the West. But enthusiastic preaching is not. And I use the word, "enthusiastic", explicitly.

The webpage at *https://www.vocabulary.com/dictionary/enthusiasm- #:~:text=The%20word%20enthusiasm%20 indicates%20intense,to%20descri* gives the following definition for the word enthusiasm:

> "The noun enthusiasm comes from the Greek word ENTHOU-SIASMOS, from ENTHOUS, meaning "possessed by a god, inspired." It was originally used in a derogatory sense to describe excessive religious zeal. Today the derogatory connotations are gone from enthusiasm, but the zeal has survived."

Observing people who witness for Christ, that is, who preach the word of his love and "saving grace", cannot but feel emotionally and religiously inspired by God to fulfill the words of the Great Commission. And why shouldn't they? It is their one great *MITSVAH*, as pointed out by Ben-Gurion.

But what about when it comes to witnessing to Jews?

When Christian missionaries talk to gentiles, they present Jesus in several roles: Savior, Son of God, and God. What do they not say to nonJews? That Jesus is the "Messiah". Messiah is a Jewish concept. It is totally meaningless to gentiles outside the so-called "Judeo-Christian" tradition. * In fact, in order to make the message of salvation universal, missionaries don't even stress that he was Jewish.

When Christian missionaries witness to Jews, however, the very first thing they mention about Jesus is that he is the Messiah for whom the Jewish People have been waiting. Jews should have recognized him as such except that they have been blinded by the hateful teaching of the Rabbis, or the TALMUD, or by their own diabolical obtuseness.

After all, Jesus himself was Jewish as were his immediate followers. The gospels record him as attending synagogue, observing Jewish religious holidays, and preaching only to Jews. In the Gospel of Matthew, he tells his disciples to preach only to Jews [Matthew 10:6 and Matthew 10:6].

When he was executed by the Romans for treason, being an enemy of the Roman Empire, a plaque was placed on his cross that read, "Jesus the Nazarene, King of the Jews."

The question haunting Christians for two thousand years is: If Jesus is the king of the Jews, why are his followers today gentiles? It is an uncomfortable question. The exclusion of the Jews from the Christian Church is seen as "a gaping hole in the body of Christ." And why is that?

One important answer to this question appears in the New Testament book, EPISTLE TO THE ROMANS, written by Paul, Christianity's creator. It is a letter to a Christian church located in Rome.

> The Remnant of Israel I ask then: Did God reject his people? By no means! God did not reject his people, whom he foreknew. So too, at the present time there is a remnant chosen by grace. What the people of Israel sought so earnestly they did not obtain. The elect among them did, but the others were hardened, as it is written: "God gave them a spirit of stupor, eyes that could not see and ears that could not hear, to this very day." (Paul seems to assemble the quote in this verse from Isaiah 29:10 and Deuteronomy 29:4) Did they stumble so as to fall beyond recovery? Not at all! Rather, because of their transgression, salvation has come to the Gentiles to make Israel envious. But if their transgression means riches for the world, and their loss means riches for the Gentiles, how much greater riches will their full inclusion bring! I take pride in my ministry in the hope that I may somehow arouse my own people to envy and save some of them. For if their rejection brought reconciliation to the world, what will their acceptance be but life from the dead? If the part of the dough offered as first fruits is holy, then the whole batch is holy; if the root is holy, so are the branches. If some of the branches have been broken off, and you, though a wild olive shoot, have been grafted in among the others and now share in the nourishing sap from the olive root, do not consider yourself to be superior to those other branches. If you do, consider this: You do not support the root, but the root supports you. You will say then, "Branches were broken off so that I could be grafted in." Granted. But they were broken off because of unbelief, and you stand by faith. Do not be arrogant. After all, if you were cut out of an olive tree that is wild by nature, and contrary to nature were grafted into a cultivated olive tree, how much more readily will these, the natural branches, be grafted into their own olive tree! All Israel Will Be Saved I do not want you to be ignorant of this mystery, brothers, and sisters, so that you may not be conceited: Israel has experienced a hardening in part until the full number of the Gentiles has come in, and in this way, all Israel will be saved. As far as the gospel is concerned, they are enemies for your sake; but as far as election is concerned, they are loved on account of the patriarchs, just as you who were at one time disobedient to God have now received mercy as a result of their disobedience, so they too have now become disobedient in order that they too may now receive mercy as a result of God's mercy to you. For God has bound everyone over to disobedience so that he may have mercy on them all.
>
> *Romans 11:1-32*

By two decades after the death of Jesus, it had become obvious that Jews were not going to recognize him as either the Messiah or anybody else religiously important. Christianity, created by Paul of the city of Tarsus, is a new rising religion among nonJews. Paul needs to explain to these gentiles why Jews are not joining them in the new faith. He explains it as God's plan to make Israel blind to the fact that their Messiah has come so that word can go out to the non-Jewish world that God's saving grace is now available to everyone. The effect will be that once Jews see that gentiles are becoming the favorites of God by their acceptance of Jesus as the savior, they (Jews) will become jealous, and then a saving remnant of Israel will eventually also become Christians.

Therefore, Christians should not think that Jews have been rejected by God. Paul calls Jews the ENEMIES of the gospel of Christ's salvation and thereby the current enemies of Christianity. But in the future, after "the full number of the Gentiles" have been converted, that will change because the Jewish People are still "loved on account of the patriarchs". That is to say, Jews appear to be loved by God because they are descendants of Abraham, not because of their own inherent self-worth, or because they follow God's commandments. No. Following the commandments of the *TORAH* is seen as a hindrance to salvation. Otherwise, God would have offered the *TORAH* to gentiles. Not only are the commandments a hindrance; they keep Jews from accepting God's "grace". MITSVOT don't save. Belief in Jesus as savior does.

Christian missionaries call Jews who have become Christian, "COMPLETED Jews "[perhaps oblivious of the insult the phrase implies, perhaps not].

The actual situation is that it is Christianity itself that is not complete. It cannot be complete unless and until the Biblical People to whom the messianic promise was made join the Church.

If, as Paul says, until Jesus' mission is completed and "ALL ISRAEL WILL BE SAVED", Jesus cannot return to initiate the Golden Age, the Age in which he is sovereign [John 18:36], then the Jews' very obstinate refusal to be converted, despite 2000 years of compulsion, is an impediment to the Christian divine plan. If expulsions, inquisitions, crusades, and a Holocaust inspired by the New Testament haven't brought Israel in, what will?

Friendly persuasion? Missionaries hope so.

* The term, "Judeo-Christian tradition" was coined by American Protestantism in the mid-20th century; its main purpose seems to have been as a political banner against post-Second World War "godless Communism". Before that time, the idea of a "Judeo-Christian" tradition was foreign to Christendom since Christianity saw itself as the successor to an inferior Judaism which it claimed to replace as the faith of a "new Israel".

> For neither is circumcision anything, nor uncircumcision, but a new creation. And as
> many as shall walk by this rule, peace be upon them, and mercy, and upon the Israel of God.
> *Galatians 6:15,16*

"The Israel of God" was understood as a synonym for the Christian Church.

THE ANTI-JEWISHNESS OF CHRISTIAN SCRIPTURE

Whatever else the New Testament is, or whatever else Christians say it is, it a polemic against Judaism, and therefore one against Jews.

Since the original Nazarenes believed that the religion of the *TORAH* was the best, so now Christians believed that the religion of the gospel was better than the very best that the world had to offer. Not only were early Christians incensed that Jews as a people were not accepting the gospel but they were equally appalled to see the Jewish religion a hard competitor among many gentiles.

Paul, the founder and chief prophet of Christianity had told his followers that:

> As concerning the gospel, they [Jews] are enemies for your sakes.
> *Romans 11:28*

No matter how Paul and his Christians may have philosophized this statement, the fact remains that "enemies" are enemies, no matter for whose sake.

The Jewish religion was long established by the time the Romans were building an empire. Rome recognized Judaism as a legal religion, allowing Jews to worship freely. Julius Caesar and Augustus supported laws that allowed Jews protection to worship as they chose. Christianity was not so lucky.

Before the fourth century CE, Christianity was forbidden by Roman law. Christians were executed and suffered other severe punishments. The Roman Empire brutally persecuted Christians for two main reasons. Firstly, it was a new and unknown religious movement. Christianity was a religion without a land or long history. Any new idea or philosophy was viewed with suspicion and seen as a threat. This is why the Romans had a policy of tolerance toward the Jewish religion. The Romans did not like Jews but Jewish civilization was old and had a homeland. The Roman Empire gave Jews an exemption from worshipping Roman gods and the emperor as long as they submitted to the political laws of Rome.

The second reason that the Romans persecuted Christians was that they regarded Christianity as a possible terrorist movement bent on the destruction of Rome. After all, the man whom Christians worshipped had been executed by Rome as an insurrectionist.

In 64CE, a major fire broke out in Rome destroying two-thirds of the city. The emperor Nero blamed the fire on the Christian community residing in Rome, initiating the first persecution of Christians.

Jewish favoritism among the Romans plus Jewish contempt for the Christian faith bred Christian hatred towards Jews.

Christians were using, actually misusing, the Jews' own scripture to prove that Jesus was the promised Anointed One and that he would be rejected by his own people. The greatest example of this is the 53rd chapter of the book of the prophet Isaiah.

He is despised and rejected of men; a man of sorrows, and acquainted with grief: and we hid as it were our faces from him; he was despised, and we esteemed him not. Surely he hath borne our griefs, and carried our sorrows: yet we did esteem him stricken, smitten of God, and afflicted. But he was wounded for our transgressions, he was bruised for our iniquities: the chastisement of our peace was upon him, and with his stripes, we are healed. All we like sheep have gone astray; we have turned everyone to his own way, and the Lord hath laid on him the iniquity of us all. Thou shalt make his soul an offering for sin.

Isaiah 53:3-6

Jews have many interpretations of these verses, among which, is that the figure described represents the Jewish People who are persecuted and martyred for the sins of humanity. Of course, it is no surprise that Christians see the wounded man as Jesus.

The fact that Jews did not have the same interpretation of verses in their own scripture that Christians had, only served to cause Christians to accuse Jews of religious ignorance, or blindness, or of obtuseness, or of a diabolically willful mean-spirited attitude towards the Christian faith.

As Christology, the idea that Jesus was the divine Christ, evolved, so did animosity towards Jews, and that animosity is embedded in the pages of the New Testament.

The animosity began with Paul's letters to the various churches he founded.

In his letter to the church at Philippi, he writes:

Beware of dogs, beware of evil workers, beware of the circumcision. For we are the circumcision, which worship God in the spirit, and rejoice in Christ Jesus, and have no confidence in the flesh. Though I might also have had confidence in the flesh. If any other man thinks that he has whereof he might trust in the flesh, I more: Circumcised the eighth day, of the stock of Israel, of the tribe of Benjamin, a Hebrew of the Hebrews; as touching the *TORAH*, a Pharisee; Concerning zeal, persecuting the church; touching the righteousness which is in the *TORAH*, blameless. But what things were gain to me, those I counted loss for Christ. Yea, doubtless, and I count all things but loss for the excellency of the knowledge of Christ Jesus my Lord: for whom I have suffered the loss of all things, and do count them but dung, that I may win Christ.

Philippians 3:2-8

This is a verbal attack on the Nazarenes who demanded that any nonJew who wished to be a follower of Jesus had to be Jewish, that is, they would have to convert to join the Nazarene Party. He warns the Philippians against any desire to be Jewish because, as he says in his letter to the Galatians,

Stand fast therefore in the liberty wherewith Christ hath made us free, and be not entangled again with the yoke of bondage. Behold, I Paul say unto you, that if ye be circumcised, Christ shall profit you nothing.

Galatians 5:1,2

But more, he himself has cast off the *TORAH* which he describes using the Greek word, SKUBALON, which literally means "shit".

In one of his earliest letters, addressed to the church at Thessalonia, he writes:

For ye, brethren, became followers of the churches of God which in Judaea are in Christ Jesus: for ye also have suffered like things of your own countrymen, even as they have of the Jews: Who both killed the Lord Jesus, and their own prophets, and have persecuted us; and they please not God, and are contrary to all men.

First Thessalonians 2:14,15

Here the arch-villains who displease God are "THE Jews." It's a blanket condemnation of all Jews. Paul uses the definite article. "The" is the equivalent of "All". Every Jew, living and dead, is described as a "Christ-killer."

Paul died in 64CE and he left a legacy of antisemitism embedded in his new faith which was faithfully picked up by the Christian leadership and drilled into the hearts and minds of the average Christian. The resultant Christian hatred of all things Jewish created a chain of events leading from Paul to the anti-Jewish laws proposed by Martin Luther to the Nazi gas chambers.

About five years after the death of Paul, an author calling himself Mark composed the first gospel incorporated into the New Testament.

Mark begins to detach Jesus from his people. Firstly there is no nativity story in Mark so there is no mention of Bethlehem, the birthplace of the Messiah. Secondly, Jesus denies the necessity of Davidic messianic ancestry. Mark presents Jesus as a boundary breaker whereas Judaism is a religion of boundaries meant to prevent Jews from living a life of chaos. Christianity, however, as we shall see in another essay, developed in a chaotic system. The boundary between Jesus and his immediate relatives is broken as is the boundary between a Jewish Davidic Messiah and whatever Mark has Jesus present himself as.

There came then his brethren and his mother, and, standing without, sent unto him, calling him. And the multitude sat about him, and they said unto him, Behold, thy mother and thy brethren without seek for thee. And he answered them, saying, Who is my mother, or my brethren? And he looked round about on them which sat about him, and said, Behold my mother and my brethren! For whosoever shall do the will of God, the same is my brother, and my sister, and mother.

Mark 3:31-35

Jesus said, while he taught in the temple, How say the scribes that Christ is the son of David? For David himself said by the Holy Ghost, The Lord said to my Lord, Sit thou on my right hand, till I make thine enemies thy footstool. David, therefore, himself calleth him Lord; and whence is he then his son?

Mark 12:35-37

Immediately thereafter, he presents the rabbis [scribes] as religious hypocrites, a theme that runs throughout the four gospels.

And he said unto them in his doctrine, Beware of the scribes, which love to go in long clothing, and love salutations in the marketplaces, And the chief seats in the synagogues, and the uppermost rooms at feasts: Which devour widows' houses, and for a pretense make long prayers: these shall receive greater damnation.

Mark 12:38-40

Not only are Jewish religious leaders devious when it comes to their religious practice but they will persecute and punish Christians for their belief in Jesus because Christians care more about saving gentiles than they do about the welfare of Jews.

But take heed to yourselves: for they shall deliver you up to councils; and in the synagogues, ye shall be beaten: and ye shall be brought before rulers and kings for my sake, for a testimony against them. And the gospel must first be published among all nations.

Mark 13:9,10

And, for no understandable reason, Jewish religious leaders want to have Jesus killed. They have nothing better to think about when they should be spending their time getting ready for an important Jewish holiday.

After two days was the feast of the Passover, and of unleavened bread: and the chief priests and the scribes sought how they might take him by craft, and put him to death.

Mark 14:1

And they happily find a collaborator among his disciples whose name is JUDAS = YEHUDAH. The name means "Jewish People".

And Judas Iscariot, one of the twelve, went unto the chief priests, to betray him unto them.

Mark 14:10

Later in the chapter, Mark reveals the reason that they want to have him killed; he calls himself the Messiah for which they charge him with blasphemy.

> The high priest asked him, and said unto him, Art thou the Christ, the Son of the Blessed? And Jesus said, I am: and ye shall see the Son of man sitting on the right hand of power, and coming in the clouds of heaven. Then the high priest rent his clothes, and saith, What need we any further witnesses? Ye have heard the blasphemy: what think ye? And they all condemned him to be guilty of death.

> *Mark 14:61-64*

Here is the Christian problem. Claiming to be the Messiah does not constitute blasphemy according to Judaism. Jews may call you delusional but no one wants to kill you. It's indicative of the major Christian problem, namely, that most Christians know nothing about Jewish history. The history that they think they know comes from the unhistorical New Testament.

Jesus is arrested by the Jewish police who then bring him before the Roman governor of Judea, Pontius Pilate. The Jewish leaders provoke a mob of angry Jews to have Pilate execute Jesus. Pilate understands that the priests are jealous of Jesus' popularity among the people and he tries to set him free but the mob calls for his crucifixion. Does any of this make logical sense? Anyone familiar with Roman history knows that Pontius Pilate was a nasty governor and a nasty individual. The Jewish historian Josephus mentions incidents of violence between the Jews of Judea and Pilate's administration. He says that Pilate acted in ways that offended the religious sensibilities of the Judeans. The Roman historian Tacitus also records this information. According to Josephus, Pilate's removal from office occurred because he ordered the massacre of a group of Samaritans protesting his abusive behavior towards them. He was sent back to Rome to answer for this incident. Although there does not seem to be a record of what happened to him after his interrogation by the Emperor, some historians believe he was exiled to Spain where he died. As one who disliked Jews and hated Jewish messianism, the last thing he would want to do is free a person calling himself the Messiah. Jesus is popular among "the people", the Jews of Judea, and yet it is they who call for his death. Why? This is the holiday of Passover and the Jews who hated the Romans and many of whom suffered Roman crucifixion have nothing better to do on this day than to call for the Roman crucifixion of a fellow Jew.

> For he [Pilate] knew that the chief priests had delivered him for envy. But the chief priests moved the people [against Jesus]. And Pilate asked them, What will ye then that I shall do unto him whom ye call the King of the Jews? And they cried out again, Crucify him.

> *Mark 15:10-12*

About the year 80CE, an author calling himself Matthew composed the second canonized gospel.

Matthew picks up the thread of anti-Jewishness begun by Mark.

He reports an incident in which a Roman military officer asks Jesus to heal one of his slaves. Jews in Galilee hated Romans more than in any other area of the Land of Israel and yet when this Roman praises Jesus for his miraculous cures, Jesus tells him that he has more faith than any Jew alive. In this gospel, it is already evident that gentiles are preferred more than Jews since it is the gentiles who will dwell with the Hebrew forefathers while Jews will be cast into the dark void.

146

And when Jesus was entered into Capernaum, there came unto him a centurion, beseeching him, And saying, Lord, my servant lieth at home sick of the palsy, grievously tormented. And Jesus saith unto him, I will come and heal him. The centurion answered and said, Lord, I am not worthy that thou shouldest come under my roof: but speak the word only, and my servant shall be healed. When Jesus heard it, he marveled, and said to them that followed, Verily I say unto you, I have not found so great faith, no, not in Israel. And I say unto you, That many shall come from the east and west and shall sit down with Abraham, and Isaac, and Jacob, in the kingdom of heaven. But the children of the kingdom shall be cast out into outer darkness.

Matthew 8:5-8,10-12

Matthew repeats the story of Jesus separating himself from his Jewish family, favoring those who worship him. That a so-called religious man should dishonor his family so, especially his mother would be considered scandalous by Jews of any generation including his.

While he yet talked to the people, behold, his mother and his brethren stood without, desiring to speak with him. Then one said unto him, Behold, thy mother and thy brethren stand without, desiring to speak with thee. But he answered and said unto him that told him, Who is my mother? and who are my brethren? And he stretched forth his hand toward his disciples, and said, Behold my mother and my brethren.

Matthew 12:46-49

Matthew repeats the story of Jesus denying that the Messiah is descended from Jewish royalty.

While the Pharisees were gathered together, Jesus asked them, Saying, What think ye of Christ? whose son is he? They say unto him, The son of David. He saith unto them, How then doth David in spirit call him Lord, saying, The Lord said unto my Lord, Sit thou on my right hand, till I make thine enemies thy footstool? If David then calls him Lord, how is he his son?

Matthew 22:41-45 [Repeated in Luke 20:41-44]

Most of chapter 23 of Matthew is filled with a diatribe against rabbis. It is too long for me to cite here but you may read the chapter at this URL:

https://www.biblegateway.com/passage/? search=Matthew%2023&version=KJV

Among the names the gentle, peace-loving Jesus calls the Jewish religious leaders are these: hypocrites, fools,, blind, and serpents, Gentle Jesus also calls down a curse upon the rabbis which makes no sense and can only be seen for the mean-spirited undeserved, senseless hatred that it is:

That upon you may come all the righteous blood shed upon the earth, from the blood of righteous Abel unto the blood of [the prophet] Zachariah.

Matthew 23:35

Many people ask why Christians have indicted the Jewish People as "Christ-killers" when according to their own theology, God Himself ordained that Jesus be killed at the Jews' behest. One answer may be found in the following verse which plainly states that although the villain has been chosen by Providence, he is still somehow guilty.

> The Son of man goeth as it is written of him: but woe unto that man by whom the Son of man is betrayed! it had been good for that man if he had not been born.
>
> *Matthew 26:24*

Mark created Jews as "Christ-killers". Matthew intensifies Jewish guilt. While Pilate, historically known to be the vicious enemy of Jews, sardonically absolves himself of any wrongdoing, the Jewish mob indicts itself for all time with a damning self-acceptance of cosmic villainy.

> Pilate saith unto them, What shall I do then with Jesus which is called Christ? They all say unto him, Let him be crucified. And the governor said, Why, what evil hath he done? But they cried out the more, saying, Let him be crucified. 24 When Pilate saw that he could prevail nothing, but that rather a tumult was made, he took water, and washed his hands before the multitude, saying, I am innocent of the blood of this just person: see ye to it. 25 Then answered all the people, and said, His blood be on us, and on our children.
>
> *Matthew 27:22-24*

But just indicting Jews for the death of Jesus is not sufficient for Matthew. Jews must also be guilty for the death of all saints from Abel to the prophets! If the author of this gospel does not sound like a madman, who does? And the gentle Jesus who asks his followers to forgive their enemies seems incapable of following his own advice. If he calls Jewish religious leaders hypocrites, then what is he?

About the year 90CE, an author calling himself Luke composed the third canonized gospel. Luke supposedly was the secretary of Paul, the founder of Christianity. His gospel uses much of the material found in Mark and Matthew.

In the third chapter of his gospel, he tells the story of Jesus going into a synagogue in his hometown of Nazareth. It appears that Jesus' purpose here is to bait and aggravate the Jews assembled there for no other reason than that they won't give him the time of day that he thinks he deserves. Angered at his insults, "the Jews" try to kill him because he keeps insinuating that gentiles are preferable to them. Early in his gospel, Luke has taken the cue from Paul that Jesus and Jews are natural enemies.

> But I tell you of a truth, many widows were in Israel in the days of Elias, when the heaven was shut up three years and six months when great famine was throughout all the land; But unto none of them was Elias sent, save unto Sarepta, a city of Sidon, unto a woman that was a widow. And many lepers were in Israel in the time of Eliseus the prophet, and none of them was cleansed, saving Naaman the Syrian. And all they in the synagogue, when they heard these

things, were filled with wrath, And rose up, and thrust him out of the city, and led him unto the brow of the hill whereon their city was built, that they might cast him down headlong.

Luke 3:25-29

Luke repeats the story of Jesus' disrespect for his Jewish family.

Then came to him his mother and his brethren, and could not come at him for the press. And it was told him by certain which said, Thy mother and thy brethren stand without, desiring to see thee. And he answered and said unto them, My mother and my brethren are these which hear the word of God, and do it.

Luke 8:19-21

Chapter ten of Luke contains the story of The Good Samaritan. This story has become so well known among Christians but they don't understand that the whole incident is an antisemitic trope.

A certain lawyer [rabbinic disciple] asks Jesus to explain to him the greatest MITSVOT. But he only asks the question to tempt Jesus into saying something negatively controversial. Jesus answers that the two great commandments are to love God and to love one's neighbor. Christians who are ignorant of the *TORAH* mistakenly believe that Jesus came up with these ideas by himself. But he is merely citing the *TORAH*. The lawyer asks him to define someone's neighbor. Luke now lets the reader know just how the lawyer is tempting him. Any knowledgeable Jew understands what Leviticus, chapter 19 is saying.

The original Hebrew of verse chapter 19, verse 18 says: "Do not seek revenge or bear a grudge against anyone among your people, but love your fellow Jew as yourself." The Hebrew word, REACH, means "ethnic brother" but Jesus expands its meaning and universalizes it. Luke, an antagonist of Jews, knows that his gospel is going to be read by gentiles. The parable shows that Jewish religious leaders callously leave the victim of robbers in his pain and distress while a hated Samaritan helps him. Luke clearly utilizes the figure of this Samaritan as a proto-Christian. What is not mentioned here is verse 33 of Leviticus 19. Unlike verses in the New Testament which encourage Christians to hate and mistreat Jews, the *TORAH* demands the opposite attitude among Jews to non-Jews. "When a foreigner [gentile] resides among you in your land, do not mistreat him. The foreigner [gentile] residing among you must be treated as your native-born. Love him as yourself, for you were foreigners in Egypt. I am the Lord your God." God will be the God of Israel if Jews follow this command.

And, behold, a certain lawyer stood up, and tempted him, saying Master, what shall I do to inherit eternal life? He said unto him, What is written in the law? how readest thou? And he answering said Thou shalt love the Lord thy God with all thy heart, and with all thy soul, and with all thy strength, and with all thy mind, and thy neighbor as thyself. And he said unto him, Thou hast answered right: this do, and thou shalt live. But he, willing to justify himself, said unto Jesus, And who is my neighbor? And Jesus answering said, A certain man went down from Jerusalem to Jericho, and fell among thieves, which stripped him of his raiment, and wounded him, and departed, leaving him half dead. And by chance there came down a certain priest that way: and when he saw him, he passed by on the other side. And likewise, a Levite, when he was at the place, came and looked on him, and passed by on the other side. But a certain Samaritan, as he journeyed, came where he was: and when he saw him, he had compassion on him, And went to him, and bound up his wounds, pouring in oil and wine, and set him on his own beast, and brought him to an inn, and took care of him. And on the morrow when he departed, he took out two pence, and gave them to the host, and said unto him, Take care of him; and whatsoever thou spendest more, when I come again, I will repay thee. Which now of these three, thinkest thou, was neighbor unto him that fell among the thieves?

Luke 10:25-36

A certain Pharisee [rabbi] invites Jesus to dinner and Jesus accepts. But he is the worst guest possible. Merely because the rabbi asks Jesus why he has not washed his hands before eating, Jesus goes into a diatribe similar to the one he delivered in Matthew 23.

And as he spake, a certain Pharisee besought him to dine with him: and he went in, and sat down to meat. And when the Pharisee saw it, he marveled that he had not first washed before dinner. And the Lord said unto him, Now do ye Pharisees make clean the outside of the cup and the platter; but your inward part is full of ravening and wickedness.

Luke 11:37-39

After cursing out his gracious host, and the rabbis, Jesus again says that Jews will have to pay for the blood of saints from Abel to Zachariah. Who knows why? Does it matter how the gospel makes Jews the villains?

And guess what? These same rabbis that Jesus has cursed out come to warn him that his life is in danger. Does he thank them? No, he tells them that the Romans will destroy Jerusalem.

The same day there came certain of the Pharisees, saying unto him, Get thee out, and depart hence: for Herod will kill thee.

Luke 13:31

O Jerusalem, Jerusalem, which killest the prophets, and stonest them that are sent unto thee; how often would I have gathered thy children together, as a hen doth gather her brood under her wings, and ye would not! Behold, your house is left unto you desolate.

Luke 13:34,35

Jesus is unhappy that animals are being sold in the Temple for sacrifice. He enters the Temple court and disrupts the sale by throwing over the tables and starting a riot. So after baiting Jewish leadership and causing a disturbance in the holy place, is it a wonder that Jewish leaders want to be rid of him?

And he went into the temple and began to cast out them that sold therein, and them that bought; Saying unto them, It is written, My house is the house of prayer: but ye have made it a den of thieves. And he taught daily in the temple. But the chief priests and the scribes and the chief of the people sought to destroy him.

Luke 19:45-47

The exoneration of Pilate and the demand by the mob that Jesus be crucified is intensified in Luke.

Pilate, therefore, willing to release Jesus, spake again to them. But they cried, saying, Crucify him, crucify him. And he said unto them the third time, Why, what evil hath he done? I have found no cause of death in him: I will therefore chastise him, and let him go. And they were instant with loud voices, requiring that he might be crucified. And the voices of them and of the chief priests prevailed.

Luke 23:20-22

About the year 100CE, an author calling himself John composed the fourth canonized gospel. Ironically, while John's gospel appears to be Christians' favorite gospel, it is also the most antisemitic. In this gospel, we are no longer dealing with Jesus the Nazarene. Here Christology has him fully evolved as Jesus Christ, both the son of God and God Himself.

In the very first chapter of his gospel, John tells the reader that Jesus "came unto his own, and his own received him not." The Christian reading this might well wonder why Jesus' own Jewish people would reject the wonderful gift of salvation he offered. Did the rabbis steer them away from Jesus or was it possibly the Devil, or both? Later on in his gospel, John has Jesus declare that THE Jews are the children of the Devil.

In chapter two of this gospel, John repeats the story of Jesus causing a riot in the Temple and disrupting the sale of sacrificial animals. In the holiest place in the Jewish religion, Jesus acting out against sacrifices betokens him replacing himself as the only rightful sacrifice in the faith meant to replace Judaism.

In chapter five of his gospel, John has Jesus indicting THE Jews for plotting to kill him in that he supposedly makes himself equal to God. But Jesus had only said that God was his father which any person could say without fear of punishment. As almost everywhere in the New Testament, Jews are referred to with the definite article, THE Jews. The definite article is equivalent to the word ALL; it means every single Jew in the world. In these verses, it is not only Jewish religious leaders who are villains but the whole Jewish People. John also has Jesus say that the reason THE Jews don't believe in him is that they don't even believe in Moses or his *TORAH*!

Therefore the Jews sought the more to kill him, because he not only had broken the sabbath but said also that God was his Father, making himself equal with God ... Do not think that I will accuse you to the Father: there is one that accuseth you, even Moses, in whom ye trust. For had ye believed Moses, ye would have believed me; for he wrote of me. But if ye believe not his writings, how shall ye believe my words?

John 5:18,45-47

151

Christians who believe in predestination, that is, that God has chosen who will be saved, probably derive that belief from the verses in chapter 6. If this is so, then the gospel is saying that God did not choose Jews to be saved.

> And he said, Therefore said I unto you, that no man can come unto me, except it were given unto him of my Father. From that time many of his disciples went back, and walked no more with him.
>
> *John 6:65,66*

But Paul had already said something similar.

> And we know that all things work together for good to them that love God, to them who are the called according to His purpose. For whom He did foreknow, He also did predestinate to be conformed to the image of his Son, that he might be the firstborn among many brethren.
>
> *Romans 8:28–29*

In chapter 7 of John's gospel, it is THE Jews rather than merely the religious leaders, who have murderous intentions towards Jesus. And it is Jesus who accuses them of not keeping the commandments of the *TORAH*.

> After these things, Jesus walked in Galilee: for he would not walk in Jewry, because the Jews sought to kill him. For neither did his brethren believe in him. When he had said these words unto them, he abode still in Galilee. But when his brethren were gone up, then went he also up unto the feast, not openly, but as it were in secret. Then the Jews sought him at the feast, and said, Where is he? ... Did not Moses give you the law, and yet none of you keepeth the law? Why go ye about to kill me? Moses, therefore, gave unto you circumcision; (not because it is of Moses, but of the fathers.
>
> *John 7:7-11,19,22*

But it is in chapter 8 that Jesus demonizes those Jews who believed in him. How can any Jew who reads this chapter still accept him as the Messiah? If this is the way he spoke to Jews who believed in him, what hope would there be for the rest of us? If Jesus calls Jews the children of the Devil and he calls the Devil the father of lies, then he is calling Jews liars. Again here, it is THE Jews who wish to kill him, not only the leaders.

> Then said Jesus to those Jews which believed in him, If ye continue in my word, then are ye my disciples indeed. They answered him, We are Abraham's seed, and were never in bondage to any man: how sayest thou, Ye shall be made free? If the Son therefore shall make you free, ye shall be free indeed. I know that ye are Abraham's seed, but ye seek to kill me because my word hath no place in you. They answered and said unto him, Abraham is our father. Jesus saith unto them, If ye were Abraham's children, ye would do the works of Abraham. But now ye seek to kill me, a man that hath told you the truth, which I have heard of God: this did not Abraham. Ye do the deeds of your father. Then said they to him, We be not born of

fornication; we have one Father, even God. Jesus said unto them, If God were your Father, ye would love me. Ye are of your father the devil, and the lusts of your father ye will do. there is no truth in him. for he is a liar and the father of it. Ye, therefore, hear not my words, because ye are not of God. Then took they up stones to cast at him but Jesus hid.

John 8:31,33,36,37,39-42,44,47,59

In chapter 10, there is a confrontation between Jesus and THE Jews at CHANNUKAH time. In these verses, Jesus tells THE Jews that he and God are one, for which THE Jews again try to kill him.

And it was at Jerusalem the feast of the dedication, and it was winter. And Jesus walked in the temple in Solomon's porch. Then came the Jews round about him, and said unto him, If thou be the Christ, tell us plainly. Jesus answered them, I told you. but ye believe not, because ye are not of my sheep. My sheep hear my voice, and I know them, and they follow me. I and my Father are one. Then the Jews took up stones again to stone him.

John 10:22-27,30,31

In chapter 11, the Jewish leaders are worried that if they allow Jesus to live and continue to do miracles enough people will proclaim him the Messiah which will cause the Romans to consider that a rebellion and they will destroy Israel. Therefore they agree that it is best to kill him rather than have the nation be killed by Rome.

Then gathered the chief priests and the Pharisees a council, and said. What do we? for this man doeth many miracles. If we let him thus alone, all men will believe in him: and the Romans shall come and take away both our place and nation. And one of them, named Caiaphas, being the high priest that same year, said unto them, Ye know nothing at all, nor consider that it is expedient for us, that one man should die for the people, and that the whole nation perishes not. And this spake he not of himself: but being high priest that year, he prophesied that Jesus should die for that nation. Then from that day forth, they took counsel together for to put him to death. Jesus, therefore, walked no more openly among the Jews but went thence unto a country near to the wilderness.

John 11:47-54

Chapter 12 tells the reader that even the belief of Jews was not good enough because they were not whole-hearted about it.

Nevertheless among the chief rulers also many believed on him; but because of the Pharisees, they did not confess him, lest they should be put out of the synagogue. For they loved the praise of men more than the praise of God.

John 12:42,43

Chapter 16 - Jesus tells his followers that Jews will throw them out of synagogues and may kill them because they don't really know God.

> They shall put you out of the synagogues: yea, the time cometh, that whosoever killeth you will think that he doeth God service. And these things will they do unto you because they have not known the Father, nor me.
>
> *John 16:2,3*

In chapter 18, Pilate interrogates Jesus as to his messianic pretensions. He also declares that it is the Jewish People who have delivered him to the Romans to be punished. Jesus' response is that THE Jews could have no power to do this unless God allowed it.

> Pilate entered into the judgment hall again, and called Jesus, and said unto him, Art thou the King of the Jews? Jesus answered him, Sayest thou this thing of thyself, or did others tell it thee of me? Pilate answered, Am I a Jew? Thine own nation and the chief priests have delivered thee unto me: what hast thou done? Jesus answered, My kingdom is not of this world: if my kingdom were of this world, then would my servants fight, that I should not be delivered to the Jews.
>
> *John 18:33-36*

I must say that I am almost embarrassed at the willful ignorance and hostility that this author has for THE Jews. In chapter 19, John puts the most outrageous words into Jewish mouths. Anyone knowing Jewish history knows Jews hated Romans for their occupation of Israel, and that they longed for a Messiah to free them from Roman dominance. But this author has the audacity to claim that this mob of Jews, with nothing better to do on the preparation day for Passover than to stand outside Pilate's home and accuse him of treason against the Emperor by sanctioning a messianic pretender. And to make things worse, THE Jews claim that Caesar is their rightful king, not an anticipated Messiah.

> And from thenceforth Pilate sought to release him: but the Jews cried out, saying, If thou let this man go, thou art, not Caesar's friend: whosoever maketh himself a king speaketh against Caesar. When Pilate, therefore, heard that saying, he brought Jesus forth and sat down in the judgment seat. And it was the preparation of the Passover, and about the sixth hour: and he saith unto the Jews, Behold your King! But they cried out, Away with him, away with him, crucify him. Pilate saith unto them, Shall I crucify your King? The chief priests answered We have no king but Caesar.
>
> *John 19*

Having covered the most significant antisemitic verses in the New Testament, I would like to end this with an insight that I read on QUORA.

You either view the crucifixion as a sacrifice or as a murder. If it was a sacrifice there's no reason to blame whoever was responsible for the sacrifice. If it was a murder, your salvation (is based on) the wages of sin, and not just any sin but the worst sin imaginable, the torturing to death of the Son of God. Calling it a murder has theological consequences. Calling it a murder makes you complicit. If you're complicit, you have no right to point fingers.

C.J. Ressler

FROM JESUS TO CHRISTIANITY: PEOPLE'S SEARCH FOR A MEANINGFUL SALVATION

Not much is known about the real human Jewish apocalyptic preacher called Jesus [YESHUA] the Nazarene. What we do know about him comes from the gospels in the New Testament. However, we have to approach the gospel accounts about him with reservations because the gospels are not history books in the sense of what we in the modern world look upon as a history book.

In effect, the gospels are stories of religious salvation brought about by a divine being, composed while the process of Christology was forming, the process of turning Jesus the Nazarene into the god Jesus Christ,

The gospels tell us that Jesus was from a Galilean town called Nazareth where he was probably born and raised. The earliest gospel, Mark, was written just after Jerusalem and the Temple were destroyed by the Romans. This happened after a five-year war provoked by Galilean Zealots in response to overly extreme taxation imposed by the Empire. Mark's gospel introduces the reader to Jesus as an adult. There is no mention of his virgin birth in the city of Bethlehem.

The reader is informed that Jesus had a trade handed down to him by his father, that of TECHTON. This Greek word is usually translated as 'carpenter' however the actual meaning of the word is something like 'handyman'. He may have been a carpenter but also may have been a metal worker or any other type of person skilled at a wide range of home repairs. If so, he wasn't doing handiwork for long.

The New Testament story tells that he was possibly a disciple of a wandering mission preacher, John the Immerser, calling upon the Jewish People to repent before the advent of the End Times when human history will end and the Golden Age known as the Kingdom of Heaven will begin. John urged Jews to immerse themselves in the water of the Jordan River in order to wash away their sins. Ritual immersion in water is practiced by Jews for several reasons such as conversion to the faith and at the completion of menstruation. One immerses oneself in a water bath known as the MIKVAH. The Kingdom of Heaven is synonymous with the Messianic Age.

At some point, Jesus separates himself from John and becomes involved with a sect called Nazarenes [NOTSRIM]. The term NOTSRIM is found in the book of Jeremiah [31:6] and is translated as 'watchmen'.

'There shall be a day, that the watchmen upon the mount Ephraim shall cry, Arise ye, and let us go up to Zion unto the Lord our God.'

The term can also be translated as 'guardians'. The question is - what were the Nazarenes guarding? The gospels make them sound like religious zealots who were preaching the coming of the Kingdom of Heaven. We don't know if they were militant zealots and we don't know if the sect existed before Jesus was part of it - but he is presented to the reader as the leader of the group, a very charismatic leader.

Jesus gathers disciples about him and in his story, 12 are chosen as special disciples who have an intimate relationship with him. He sends these 12 out to preach to Jews and to practice faith healing and exorcism in his name.

As stated, it is uncertain if the Nazarenes were a militant sect, but consider this. One of Jesus' disciples is called Simon the Zealot. The Zealots were a strong militant, anti-Roman group in Galilee, and apparently this Simon was drawn to the sect by the charisma of Jesus. There were also two other disciples, brothers John and James, whom the gospels refer to as "Sons of Thunder" [Mark 3:17] Luke's gospel speaks of an occasion in which the people in a Samaritan village respond negatively to Jesus and his message; it is these Sons of Thunder who ask Jesus to call down fire from heaven on them [Luke 9:54]. The Jews of Galilee were the most violently anti-Roman, and eventually provoked the war with Rome which ended with the destruction of Jerusalem and the Temple. That the Galilean Nazarenes may have been a militant group should not surprise us.

Developed Christianity describes Jesus as meek and peaceful. The gospels show another side of him.

> Do not think that I have come to bring peace to the earth. I have not come to bring peace, but a sword. For I have come to set a man against his father, and a daughter against her mother, and a daughter-in-law against her mother-in-law. And a person's enemies will be those of his own household.
>
> *Matthew 10:34-36*

This is quite far from the "family values" preached by modern Christians.

> I have come to send fire on the earth; and how I wish it were already kindled. Suppose ye that I have come to give peace on earth? I tell you, Nay; but rather division.
>
> *Luke 12:49,51*

It seems that he has become more proactive in his mission to usher in the Kingdom of Heaven, the Messianic Age.

During the last week of his life, the gospels tell a story that in Christianity is called the Cleansing of the Temple. Jesus is described as entering the Temple Court and overturning the tables of the money changers. This happens a few days before a pilgrim holiday. The gospels have it be Passover, but there are New Testament scholars who believe it was Tabernacles [SUKKOT].

If the Cleansing of the Temple has any historical validity, then it underplays a more serious breach of the peace. New Testament scholars believe that the Nazarenes actually took over the Temple and forced the Jewish and Roman authorities out. And this was probably one act in a wider insurrection against Rome.

Luke, chapter 23 describes a freedom fighter named Barabbas who was arrested in an insurrection

[The people cry out]"release unto us Barabbas who was cast into prison for a certain insurrection made in the city, and murdered [Romans]."

Ultimately the insurrection is quashed by the Romans and the ring leaders, including Jesus, are arrested and put on trial for treason against the Roman Empire.

Jesus' situation becomes more perilous than the other insurrectionists when people begin to hail him as the "Anointed One" [MESHIACH], that is, the long-awaited, King Messiah. We cannot know for certain whether or not Jesus believed himself to be the Messiah but certainly he must have believed that he was somehow someone ushering in the Golden Age. But even if he did not say that he was the Messiah, very shortly after his death, his followers are calling him that.

Jesus is tried by the Jewish and Roman authorities and found guilty of rebellion against the Roman Empire. He, along with two other men, is executed by crucifixion.

> And there were also two other malefactors [KAKOURGOI] led with him to be put to death.
> *Luke 23:32*

This Greek word, KAKOURGOS, means "violent criminal", not "thief". It's a word that the Romans used to describe rebels, equivalent to our word, "terrorist".

Given that Jesus' band of followers seized the Temple court, that an insurrectionist named Barabbas was somehow involved, and that two "freedom fighters" were executed alongside Jesus, we may conclude that Jesus and the Galilean Nazarenes were not merely peaceful apocalyptic "Guardians"; on the contrary, they were militant, and Jesus as their leader paid the ultimate price for his messianic aspirations. The sign on his cross read, "JESUS THE NAZARENE, KING OF THE JEWS". Whether or not he thought of himself in that role, the Romans certainly saw him as a Jewish royal pretender.

Jesus' disciples in the Nazarene sect must have felt a loss at the death of their master, and a deep disappointment in that he failed to bring in the Messianic Age. His charismatic leadership and his faith healings must have convinced them that he was indeed the Messiah long awaited by the Jewish People. How was it possible that the Roman enemy had taken his life? Still convinced that he had been the promised one, they sought a reason that would make theological sense. And that reason shortly occurred to them. Some of his followers believed that he had successfully raised a man from the dead. If he had the power to do that for another individual, then certainly he had the power to raise himself from the dead. But why suffer death at all other than to show the Roman enemy that even if they did their worst to him, namely kill him but fail to keep him in the grave, then all the world would know that he was indeed an undefeatable anointed messianic king who would return to usher in the Kingdom of Heaven.

Soon after his death, his disciples returned to Galilee in disappointment but shortly his followers began to report seeing visions of him and the tales of these visions convinced those who loved him that he had indeed returned to them from the grave. The belief in his return caused his followers to return to Jerusalem from Galilee to wait for what they believed would be his imminent second coming.

It appears that his disciples chose his brother James as their new leader. They daily frequented the Temple court, speaking to Jews who would hear that the Messiah had come and was coming back to initiate the Golden Age. They gained adherents perhaps by telling of great miracles that Jesus had performed and would again perform for those who accepted him as the Messiah. But they felt no disdain or negativity towards those who refused to believe.

This group of Nazarenes is often referred to as the Jerusalem Church but it was no such thing. A church, by definition, is an institution. Institutions require two things to perform; a hierarchy and a mission. James' group had neither. The group had no hierarchy of priests, bishops, cardinals, or any such. Neither had it a mission. They appealed to passersby by persuasion but there was no active proselytizing. Whatever "mission" they might have engaged in was to preach to Jews of the Land of Israel.

This simplicity of persuasion worked until the advent of the major Jewish holidays which brought diaspora pilgrims to Jerusalem. The New Testament book, ACTS OF THE APOSTLES, tells of an epiphany that occurred on the festival of Pentecost [SHAVUOT] where a group of Israeli and diaspora Jews were worshipping together and experienced some sort of divine inspiration which caused them to speak a mystical tongue, a spiritual manifestation of the presence of Jesus. The messianic message of James' Nazarenes now became a belief among Greek-speaking diaspora Jews who changed that message into a mission, complete with a hierarchy of deacons, and ministers ranking below that of rabbis or priests.

Whatever the diaspora pilgrims were told about Jesus by his Israeli followers, they were sufficiently impressed to bring the news of a resurrected messiah back to their respective home cities. Greek being their native tongue, they told their fellow Jews about Iesus Xristos, Jesus the Anointed. This charismatic message about an invincible Jewish king generated sufficient excitement so that the message spread among the congregations in the diaspora synagogues.

At the time of the first century of the Common Era, in the diaspora, many gentiles had become attracted to the Jewish religion, something encouraged by many diaspora Jews. This did not mean that these gentiles converted to become Jews but simply that they began to take up Jewish practices and familiarize themselves with the Greek translation of the *TORAH*. This translation is called the Septuagint, abbreviated LXX. Those gentiles who did convert were mostly women who didn't have to undergo the difficult procedure of circumcision. Children of these converted women were raised as Jews since they were Jewish according to Jewish law, being born of Jewish mothers. Gentiles attracted to the religion of Israel who did not officially convert were known in Hebrew as YIREI *HASHEM*, "those who stand in awe of God" or simply "God-Fearers."

Word of the expected Kingdom of Heaven soon to be brought to earth by the Anointed Iesous Xristos attracted more diaspora Jews; many of these Jews began to believe that their God-Fearing gentile neighbors ought to be part of the Nazarene community and these gentiles began to be actively proselytized.

When news of this activity got back to James and the Nazarene group in Jerusalem, it was accompanied by a feeling of discomfort. The disciples in leadership, James the brother of Jesus, Simon Peter, Jesus' supposed chosen lieutenant, and John, one of the "Sons of Thunder" felt that the Nazarene message was meant only for Jews. According to the gospels, Jesus had always told his disciples to go only to Jews and avoid gentiles.

Matthew 10:5,6 "These twelve Jesus sent forth, and commanded them, saying, Go not into the way of the Gentiles, and into any city of the Samaritans enter ye not: But go rather to the lost sheep of the house of Israel."

But Jews in the Greek-speaking diaspora felt friendlier to non-Jews than Jews living in Israel, and encouraged their gentile friends to live according to the *TORAH*. And the Jews who believed Jesus to be the messiah encouraged this belief among gentiles.

Emboldened by belief in a risen messiah who would soon return to overthrow the Roman Empire and establish the kingdom of Heaven, diaspora Nazarenes, and other militant messianic Jews began to employ terrorist acts of violence against the Romans, possibly encouraged by apocalyptic writings such as the book of Revelation which became the final book in the New Testament. This prompted Jewish and Roman authorities in Israel to send out police and bounty hunters to arrest messianic troublemakers. It seems as though groups of these messianists congregated in the city of Damascus in Syria.

A man named Saul from the city of Tarsus, located in what is now south-central Turkey, was recruited by the Jewish authorities as either a policeman or a bounty hunter and was sent to Damascus to find and arrest messianists in that city. On his way to Damascus, he is reported to have experienced some sort of epiphany. New Testament scholars are not sure about the historicity of this epiphany but the New Testament book of Acts of the Apostles describes it as follows:

> And Saul, yet breathing out threatenings and slaughter against the disciples of the Lord, went unto the high priest, And desired of him letters to Damascus to the synagogues, that if he found any of this way, whether they were men or women, he might bring them bound unto Jerusalem. And as he journeyed, he came near Damascus: and suddenly there shined round about him a light from heaven: And he fell to the earth and heard a voice saying unto him, Saul, Saul, why persecutest thou me? And he said, Who art thou, Lord? And the Lord said: I am Jesus whom thou persecutest. And he trembling and astonished said, Lord, what wilt thou have me to do? And the Lord said unto him, Arise, and go into the city, and it shall be told thee what thou must do.
>
> *Acts 9:1-6*

What this story means is hard to say but it is evident that Saul experienced something psychologically emotional so as to convert him from a persecutor of messianists to a follower of Jesus the Nazarene.

> And there was a certain disciple at Damascus, named Ananias; and to him said the Lord in a vision, Ananias. And he said, Behold, I am here, Lord. And the Lord said unto him, Arise, and go into the street which is called Straight, and enquire in the house of Judas for one called Saul, of Tarsus: for, behold, he prayeth, And hath seen in a vision a man named Ananias coming in, and putting his hand on him, that he might receive his sight. Then Ananias answered, Lord, I have heard by many of this man, how much evil he hath done to thy saints at Jerusalem.
>
> *Acts 9:10-13*

In Saul's speech in Acts 22, he describes Ananias as "a devout man according to the *TORAH*, having a good report of all the Jews" that dwelt in Damascus (Acts 22:12).

Early in Christianity, probably by some time in the second Christian century, the doctrine of the Trinity emerged. The doctrine asserts that God exists as three persons but is still one God. The persons in the Trinity Godhead are God the Father, God the Son [Jesus Christ], and God the Holy Spirit. Each of these persons has a different and specific role to play in history. The Father is the divine aspect that created the universe; the Son emerged from the Father and his role is to bring humanity into a perfect relationship with the Father by becoming human and sacrificing himself by dying and rising.

According to this view, mankind is too impure to interact with the Father directly but mankind can interact with God as a fellow human being. Trinitarianism maintains that God as Christ is the Jewish Messiah prophesied by the Hebrew scriptures. The Holy Spirit is the divine presence that communicates revelations to humanity.

In the third Christian century, a Christian priest named Arius from Alexandria, Egypt said that Christ was not God; he was created by God to be His son and was therefore not the equal of God nor coeternal with Him.

By the fifth century CE, in Syria, Egypt, and Anatolia [modern Turkey], the doctrine of monophysitism arose. The Monophysites claimed that Jesus was God, pure and simple. They based their belief on Jesus saying many times in the gospels, that he and the Father were one. Therefore Monophysites denied the doctrine of the Trinity.

Somewhere around the first Christian century and continuing on for a few hundred years, educated and intelligent people in the Roman Empire began thinking of monotheism as the only logical religious outlook. The idea of a plurality of gods, most of whom did not conduct themselves with any degree of morality or integrity, began to seem unreasonable. Some pagans in the Empire might have been influenced by Judaism or the growing faith of Christianity, but that did not mean that Romans would adopt either one of these religions. These pagan monotheists saw the old Roman gods as concretized expressions of the various attributes of the One Unknown All-Powerful Deity. They were thereby primed to accept Christianity as the true articulation of their belief in a single God. This faith's God was at once supreme and unknowable and yet human and available to the ordinary person.

During the reign of the Roman Emperor Constantine, CE 306–337, Christianity had become the numerically dominant religion of the Roman Empire. In 313, Constantine decriminalized Christian worship and the persecution of Christians by the Romans State came to an end. During one of his military campaigns the year prior, Constantine reported seeing a vision of a cross in the sky, and attached to it the words, BY THIS SIGN YOU WILL CONQUER. After winning the battle, he took it as an indication that the Christian God had spoken to him and granted him victory.

Constantine may have felt that the Empire would be strengthened by wedding it to one faith for all Romans rather than the plethora of gods that each was worshipping. But since there were different versions of his new faith, he wished to establish an orthodoxy. In 325, he summoned the bishops of the various differing beliefs about Jesus to the Greek city of Nicaea located in Anatolia [modern Turkey] to attempt to define orthodoxy for the whole Church. The Trinitarian view was adopted as Christian orthodoxy.

Starting in 324, Constantine began building a new city, New Rome, at Byzantium in Anatolia, and he named it Constantinople, the city of Constantine. Unlike the original Rome, Constantinople was built as a specifically Christian city with no temples from other religions. By the end of his reign, he had begun to order the tearing down of pagan temples in Rome. Despite the fact that the Council of Nicaea preferred a doxology wherein God and Christ are one, Constantine was baptized only on his deathbed by the Arian bishop Eusebius of Nicomedia in 337.

In 380, the emperor Theodosius issued an edict which made Christianity, Nicene Christianity, the official religion of the Roman Empire.

Still if anyone believed that the Council of Nicaea could resolve the issue of who Jesus Christ was, that individual was mistaken. The Monophysites and the Arians continued to hold on to their views of Christ, and continued to propagate those views among their people.

From the fourth through the sixth centuries, bloody wars erupted between the proponents of the conflicting views of Jesus. Each believed that God was angry with those who held the wrong beliefs and that He would punish them with sickness, plague, famines, floods, and worse. During these centuries, the infighting became so intense that the Eastern Roman provinces of Eqypt and Syria, and the city of Constantinople weakened, and the center of Christian gravity shifted to Europe. Former European provinces of the Empire were becoming independent kingdoms loyal to the bishop of Rome who elevated himself to the position of Father [Pope] of Western Christianity. The military of the Western Empire, being stronger than those of the East, succeeded in slaughtering more fellow Christians than its Eastern competitors, and doctrine of the Trinity became Universal [Catholic] Christianity. When the Western Empire fell in 476, the Pope became, for all practical purposes, the unacknowledged emperor of a Christianized Catholic Europe.

But even after all that, underground heresies continued to come into existence and when eventually discovered, their adherents were put to death. In the name of the gentle, peaceful Jesus, untold numbers of pagans, innocent women [accused of witchcraft], Jews, and fellow Christians were burnt at the stake. These atrocities performed by so-called Christian men of good will continued until the dawn of the modern era when most governments ceased being run by kings and clergy, and became more or less secular. Once ordinary citizens no longer feared the wrath of the clergy, heresies began to reappear.

In the 16th century, the heresy of Protestantism appeared in England and in German-speaking lands and quickly spread over northern Europe. The Papacy could not contain it. Although Protestants did away with the outward forms of Catholicism, they kept the belief in the Trinity. And in more recent times monophysitism reappeared in the form of Pentecostalism, and Arianism reappeared in the form of Jehovah's Witnesses.

It appears that in the 21st century, the center of Christian gravity is moving to the global south - Africa and South America, and in these areas, Pentecostalism is rising among the poorer classes. Pentecostalism may someday become the new Orthodoxy, replacing the Orthodox belief in the Trinity.

Having said all this, Christians, and all who join them, are left with this difficulty. Christians believe that two thousand years ago, God, the Creator of the universe, came to a young woman named Miriam living in a small, insignificant town in an unimportant province at the edge of the Roman Empire, and there, with the Virgin Mary, sired someone later called Jesus Christ whose precise identity his worshippers have never been able to agree about.